CLOUGHIE

WALKING ON WATER

MY LIFE
BRIAN CLOUGH

with John Sadler

This publication constitutes an exclusive abridgement for
FourFourTwo magazine. The full commemorative edition is
published by Headline Book Publishing, priced £18.99

headline

First published in 2002
by HEADLINE BOOK PUBLISHING

First published in paperback in 2003
by HEADLINE BOOK PUBLISHING

This edition produced specially for *FourFourTwo* in 2005

10 9 8 7 6 5 4 3 2 1

ISBN 0 7553 1411 5

Typeset in Ehrhardt by Letterpart Limited, Reigate, Surrey
Text design by Ben Cracknell Studios
Printed and bound in Great Britain by
Mackays of Chatham plc, Chatham, Kent

Papers and cover board used by Headline are natural, recyclable
products made from wood grown in sustainable forests.
The manufacturing processes conform to the environmental
regulations of the country of origin.

HEADLINE BOOK PUBLISHING
A division of Hodder Headline
338 Euston Road
LONDON NW1 3BH

www.headline.co.uk
www.hodderheadline.com

CHAPTER 1

A HARD LIFE AND A SOUND SENSE OF VALUES

I didn't go into coaching with any particular precon-
ceived ideas or theories. I didn't go into it convinced I
would become one of the best managers who ever drew
breath. I went into it as a former centre-forward with
one of the best goalscoring records of all time who was
scandalously disregarded and under-used by his country – two bloody caps for a lad who was totting up goals
like telephone numbers. I was overlooked mainly
because Walter Winterbottom preferred a player called
Derek Kevan, a big, bruiser of a player from West Brom
who scored a goal or two here and there but wasn't in
my class, nowhere near it.

Apart from the two full caps, this is my international
record: one England B cap and one goal; three appearances for the Under-23 side and another goal; two

games for the Football League representative team – six goals; one game for an FA XI – five goals. That's right, five in one game for the second time in a representative shirt, and I'd achieved it once for Middlesbrough as well, against Brighton in my fourth season.

I didn't go into coaching because of my record as a player but because I needed a job, needed the money and needed a future.

It was the past that armed me. I wasn't aware of it then, but I'm sure now. The sudden and premature end of my playing days had an important subconscious effect. I would make damned sure that every footballer with whom I came into contact made the most of whatever ability he had. If he didn't, he wouldn't remain in my company for very long. The ability to play football for your living, or any sport for that matter, is a gift that should be cherished and relished by those who have it. Those who abuse it to the extent that they reduce their capacity to perform at their very best are guilty of a criminal waste.

I knew how much I was envied by the supporters of Middlesbrough and Sunderland. First I was the local lad made good and when I moved from one to the other I was still aware of the warmth and friendship despite arriving at Roker from one of their fiercest rivals. I would have hated to be transferred further afield. I couldn't have gone to a London club, for instance. That would have been like moving to a different country. It seemed so far away, and struck me as a vast, impersonal place, too big to be intimate and cosy. Of course, people who were born there and who live there will probably argue the opposite, but I would have been homesick within days.

The Northeast was home to me, an area that still regards itself as out on its own as far as football is concerned. The people have a parochial mentality, in the nicest possible sense, and their love of football is more intense than it is anywhere else in England. If one of the three major clubs, Newcastle, Sunderland or Middlesbrough, had had the success of Manchester United, Arsenal or Liverpool, they wouldn't be playing to crowds of 67,000 nowadays; they'd need grounds big enough to hold 167,000.

I was just like the fans who paid their hard-earned money to watch – consumed by the game. Other places didn't interest me, apart from their football grounds. Every city seems pretty much the same to footballers. There's not much difference between a trip to one railway station and hotel and a trip to another. Playing was everything.

There were a lot of northern clubs in the second division. We seemed to be playing in Rotherham, Barnsley, Huddersfield or Doncaster every other week. For a while, the furthest I travelled was Nottingham. I scored my first hat-trick at the City Ground in 1956. These days in the Premiership, there are plenty of foreign players with glamorous names – Laurent Blanc, Thierry Henry, Dennis Bergkamp, Juan Sebastian Veron, Jimmy Floyd Hasselbaink, Kanu, Ruud Van Nistelrooy. There was something so much more homely and comfortable, simpler and more straightforward, about the names of those we played against, Barnsley's goalkeeper Harry Hough, for instance. You can't go wrong with a Harry Hough. You don't expect any more than he can give from a man called Harry Hough. As you might imagine, he was as tough as a tree, solid as a rock – that I can vouch for because, as a centre-forward, I know that when he clattered you there was no room for doubt; you had the bruises to remind you for weeks.

Charlie Williams is another name to conjure with. He might not have had the style of a Laurent Blanc but as one of the first coloured players in our game, he had more to prove than the Frenchman who joined Manchester United so late in his distinguished career. Charlie inevitably attracted a lot of attention well before he went on stage as a comic. He wasn't a bad player, either – a terrific athlete and game as a pebble. On one occasion when we played Doncaster, Charlie didn't give me a kick – apart from the ones he landed around my shins and calves. 'I'm going wherever you go,' he said. He stuck so tight that I told him, 'If you come any closer to me we might as well get into the same pair of shorts and save a few bob on laundry.'

Doncaster's goalkeeper Harry Gregg, another good, solid name, was an international with Northern Ireland. He later joined Manchester United and was among the lucky ones to survive the Munich disaster. In one game at Ayresome Park I'd stuck a couple past him and he was frantic. He charged out to the edge of the penalty area, foaming at the mouth, and screamed at me, 'You come anywhere near this box again and you'll not get out alive.' He'd completely lost it, couldn't take it, but his Irish charm was never far below the surface and after the game his was the first arm to be draped around my shoulder in friendship as we left the pitch.

Football was such an important part of the lives of people in the Northeast that even amateur football was renowned. Bishop Auckland used to win the Amateur Cup at Wembley season after season. In their way, Bishop Auckland were as famous as the rest of the Northeastern teams, and I'm including the times when Jackie Milburn was a folk hero at Newcastle and when Wilf Mannion was regarded as a god at Ayresome Park. They used to talk about 'hotbeds' of football, the areas of the country where young talent could be found in abundance. South Yorkshire was one but no bed was hotter than the Northeast. We regarded ourselves as the Mecca of the game and allowed the Londoners to delude themselves by thinking they were the important ones who ran the show.

Home games in the Northeast – and at most other venues – were staged in front of a sea of flat caps. Look at the pictures from those days. I can imagine local papers running a competition – spot a fan without a cap and win yourself ten bob. We didn't mix with supporters on a regular basis apart from on matchdays. We bumped into them in the street or the local caff from time to time but we didn't booze with them. We didn't fight with them either, which might be a surprise to some young footballers I could mention today. Football was a way of life, almost a branch of religion, in my world. Supporters would forgive you almost anything just as long as they saw you working your balls off, prepared to sweat blood for their team.

It might sound like a statement of the obvious but I was at home in the Northeast. The feeling of warmth and comfort and being needed was a continuation of the security I experienced at number 11, Valley Road, I suppose. I didn't go sightseeing before away games. For a start, there was never time and I was not one for the cultural things in life. When I was away there was only one place I wanted to be – back at home.

That pull was never greater than during an England Under-23 trip abroad in 1957. Moscow was part of the itinerary, and a conducted tour of that imposing, historic city was included. It was a privilege, of course, although few of us in the party appreciated that side of it. Bobby Charlton, my room-mate, had warned me in advance that I wouldn't fancy the food in that neck of the woods and told me to pack a lot of chocolate. I soon found out what he meant and was grateful. They might have learned how to goose-step in Russia but they had nothing to touch my mam's stew and savoury dumplings. I'd shown Bobby all about bird's-nesting in the grounds of the hotel in England before we headed for the Iron Curtain. By coincidence, the first thing I ate in Moscow was a clear soup the colour of washing-up water with a raw egg in the bottom of the bowl. I don't know what bird had laid it but at a time like that, a bar of chocolate sounds like a bloody good idea.

Not many things about Moscow registered, not the famous things that attract so many people. But I do remember being struck by the sight of so many queues. People queued for everything. They were still queuing to take a look at Lenin and he'd been dead for years. They left me out of the side to play Russia so I wasn't the happiest tourist anyway. My thoughts didn't turn to the Kremlin or anywhere else in the eastern bloc. I was fed up and wanted to go home.

They say home is where the heart is and mine was steeped in the Northeast. They made sure you kept things in perspective there. At Middlesbrough, one player had a car when Barbara and I got engaged. Lindy Delapenha was the star with the Ford Anglia and it wasn't just a gesture when he offered to take us to Stockton-on-Tees to buy the ring. It was the equivalent of giving me a knighthood, even though as I got out of the car to head for H. Samuel's, one of the doors fell off.

David Beckham, Steven Gerrard, Michael Owen and the rest of them have their cars, their 'image rights', their agents and investments, and I'm glad the game is rewarding its top performers well – but it's too well by a mile in many cases. That's not the players' fault. It's down to the chairmen and those who run the clubs who think they can keep on paying out more and more. One day soon they'll have to put a lid on it. I look at these talented and extremely fortunate young men and wonder whether, somewhere along the line, they were denied the chance to develop a proper sense of values.

They can't know what money is worth because they have too much of it. You need to be a very level-headed young man indeed, or to have enjoyed a sound and secure upbringing, if you're to cope with millionaire status before the age of twenty.

You see many leading young players on television these days and I don't mean on 'Match of the Day' or 'The Premiership'. You see them in commercials for which I assume they're paid another fortune. Whether they're advertising shampoo, sunglasses, cars or frozen peas, there's rarely a hair out of place. I don't think we were quite as fussy about our image in my day. I was a big name at Middlesbrough and at Sunderland – goal-scorers always were and I did it as well as anybody ever had – but the sea-coal still had to be gathered. I used to cycle down to Seaburn with a sack and a rake to collect coal that had been washed in by the tide. It was a cold job when that east wind blew through to your bones, and hard graft. But the coal was free and available, and the knowledge that once it was dry it would keep my mam and dad warm was incentive and reward enough, never mind the image or the reputation. Such trivial things never dawned on us. Life was harder then, the basic essentials not easy to come by or taken for granted, but it seemed so much more fulfilling on the strength of it.

This was the background, the life and the learning process, that swept me into the coaching side of foot-ball. Now I can see that I was a young man who, in the words of John Osborne, looked back in anger – a lot of anger and good reason for it. I needed a job. I had to work for a living. As my mam had instilled into me, I would make the best of it and do the job to the utmost of whatever ability might be in there, but I hadn't a clue whether I'd be good, bad or a complete and utter failure.

In quiet, reflective moments, I wonder what experiences I drew on and relied on, what lessons I'd learned from other managers that stood me in good stead and I have come to realise there were a few. I certainly learned something from Bob Dennison at Middlesbrough. It wasn't what he had or hadn't said or done; it was that he'd been hopeless – couldn't have spotted a diamond in a diamond mine. He was surrounded by jewels in the dressing room and on the training ground, international players with a lot of caps and others who were good enough to be internationals but were never given the chance – and me with my forty goals a season, regular as clockwork.

It wasn't as if he had to go out and test his judgement with a few signings – a part of the job that often dictates whether you succeed or fail, and nine times out of ten is the main reason for managers getting the sack. The talent was there for Dennison, give or take a transfer here and there. I doubt if the entire side cost anything like £100,000, but he didn't do anything with that squad of players because he didn't bung up the leaks. He needed to stop up the great big hole he had in his bucket. Points were flooding out of it. We had the ability to score goals by the boatload but Dennison did nothing about our serious problem of conceding just as regularly. No matter what was poured into that bucket of his, it was all allowed to gush out at the bottom. We couldn't defend to save our lives.

Dennison had been a defender in his time. You'd have thought he would recognise the problem, and even if he didn't know the underlying reason, it was his duty as manager to try to put it right. The need for a team to defend effectively was like a message imprinted on my mind from those infuriating days. Dennison taught me by accident, through incompetence. I learned what not to do.

The first lessons I absorbed came from Harry Storer. Anybody who knows me or has read about my career must realise how much I valued the words I heard from him. Pete Taylor, who'd had him as his manager at Coventry, introduced us when we were at Middlesbrough. A wiry little bugger he was, with a tough reputation. Most people refer to me as a talker, somebody who never stops going on. Well, I've got news for them – I was always a good listener, still am. I was a wee bit apprehensive about Storer, realising that with him it was better to be seen and rarely heard. I was awestruck but fascinated as old Harry reeled off home truths about football: 'Once you're a manager, if it ever happens, do a quick check before away games. Look at your players prior to the coach leaving and count the hearts. If there are less than five, don't bother setting off. A team's no good without courage.

'Something to remember about football club directors – whatever you do for them, as a player or a manager, you'll be lucky if you ever hear them say thank you.

'Once you're a manager, everything lands on your doorstep. If a fan trips up on his way into the ground, if a player gets barracked from the terraces, if a seat doesn't work properly, if a season-ticket holder can't find a programme seller, if the postman brings a sackful of letters saying the team's no bloody good – it will all end up in the manager's office. You can stake your life on it.'

Every word Storer said to me was eventually borne out in reality. He managed Birmingham in his time and was at Derby prior to my predecessor, Tim Ward. He might have been of the old school but former players going into management would do well to bear in mind the philosophies of Harry Storer, even today, because they still apply. Some things never change. Good advice is always good advice.

Alan Brown taught me about discipline. I knew plenty about that from my mam, of course, but Browny's discipline was applied to the team as a whole as well as to the individual. It was collective discipline. If you need an example, remember how my teams at Derby and Nottingham Forest went about their work – not by effing and blinding at match officials, not by intimidating referees or hacking the ball away in disgust at free-kicks given against us. Referees regarded my teams as their favourites because we simplified their jobs. We made refereeing easier than it was with other teams. We didn't antagonise them or chase them with angry words and gestures. That seems to be a lesson Arsene Wenger's Arsenal side has yet to learn. I don't care what they've won – they'd be respected a great deal more if they'd won it with an attitude and level of behaviour in keeping with their undoubted talent. As far as I'm concerned, they leave a nasty taste.

Brown was totally in charge at Sunderland. The first day I turned up at Roker Park, I realised he ran every aspect of the show, morning till night, top to bottom. This really was the boss at work, the gaffer who left nobody in the slightest doubt about who was in charge. I don't scare easily and never did but I remember times when I was frightened of Alan Brown. A bollocking from him was like ten from anybody else. When he dressed you down you stood there feeling totally naked. Talk about tearing you off a strip – he could tear off your entire shirt.

I often think of Browny. He's dead now, God bless him. I can be in the garden or sipping a cup of coffee or looking for relief from the boredom of a televised match when nothing is happening. Whatever the moment, I can catch a glimpse of him standing there, his back as straight as a goalpost. I can remember, as if it was today, looking at him at Sunderland and thinking to myself, 'This is the way I'll do the job if the opportunity ever comes.'

I'd seen both extremes – Dennison, easygoing and negligent when it came to repairing the suspect department of his team, and Brown, the rigid disciplinarian who allowed nothing and no one to escape his notice. Browny struck me as a fifty-year-old who wanted to be twenty. He'd been in the Guards and it showed in his magnificent physique, hard as nails and without a sign of fat, and his short, military haircut. He was not outwardly compassionate at all. He had what I had but couldn't recognise in myself at that time – terrible conceit. He used to stride down the corridors thinking he was the most important man on earth. I used to do it not realising I was doing it, but he was well aware of himself. He meant it.

Then he went to a real extreme. He introduced the entire dressing room to a man with glorious silver-grey hair, a former cricketer. He was Browny's new friend and mentor, apparently. Our gaffer had gone religious. He'd joined up with an organisation called Moral Rearmament. He wanted to get me involved and the three of us met on a couple of occasions but their jargon had me nodding off within minutes.

Browny took it seriously. Once you joined up you had to purge yourself of all your sins – confess to everything you'd done wrong in your life. I gather it took him quite some time! They used to insist they were not a religious sect but that's how I regarded them. It left the Sunderland dressing room aghast when he told us he had enrolled. Suddenly the Iron Man, as he loved us to call him, had begun to bend. Somebody once told me, 'Don't be fooled by Browny. He'll give you all the stuff about living right and not stepping out of line but he's been knocking off his secretary for eighteen months.' I'm told he admitted it when he joined MR.

Maybe a touch of compassion did enter his life once he'd joined the gang. After treatment on my injured knee one afternoon, he offered me a lift home. He installed me and my plaster cast across the back seat of his car and when we arrived at my house he just said, 'Get on my back.' He piggy-backed me to my front door and told me to stand on my good leg and lean against the wall while he fetched my crutches from the boot. 'See you tomorrow,' he said as he handed them to me. Nothing else. Alan Brown was not one to talk a lot.

I'm grateful to him because, without realising it, he sent me into management with his conceit and arrogance and the highest possible regard for discipline in a football club. He lacked that human touch that warms a man's personality. I used to think he was someone who hadn't been conceived – he'd been constructed.

Taking those first steps up the coaching and management ladder, I knew I wanted to be strict. I wanted to be arrogant and by then I knew I was conceited because I was born conceited. So although I was dipping my big toe into unfamiliar waters that first morning George Hardwick let me work with Sunderland's youth players, I had an air of confidence about me. It was well founded because, would you believe, the moment I got out the practice balls and gathered those young footballers together and started to talk, I discovered straightaway that I had another ability to my name. I could teach.

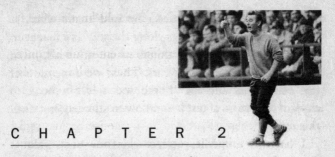

CHAPTER 2

HEY, I CAN MANAGE

It's only when you get on in years that you fully appreciate how it all happened – in my case, how a raggy-arsed slip of a lad from a big family in Middlesbrough, with a big head and talented feet, made it and became a name known to millions. Bad luck, or fate, put paid to my playing days before I had the chance to do full justice to myself but nobody needs reminding of my achievements in management with Derby and Nottingham Forest. They are there for all to see. They are in the record books, in black and white, and I've talked and written about them often enough to make sure nobody forgets.

It's why I was so successful, how it happened, that intrigues me, and it should intrigue every young man who fancies his chances as a manager and every manager already working but still wondering why he's not succeeding. That's why I've dwelt so long on my upbringing and playing career because that's where it came from. I learned things along the way as a manager, obviously, but there were things inside my head, often little things that stuck for years. These were the roots of my managerial success. There was never a book to explain how to go about it and how to succeed, not until this one.

I had an immediate effect on the youth side at Sunderland. I was with them for just one season but they started winning matches virtually straight away. There are two things to say about that. Firstly, they all looked up to me as the best centre-forward, or former centre-forward, in the country, so I was given instant and total respect. As you might imagine, that appealed to me. Conceited men like to be looked up to. Secondly, I changed the training. They didn't spend their time jogging lap after lap around the training ground; they spent almost all the session with a ball.

Training was regimented, predictable and boring when I started out as a professional player. Maybe that was another reason why Middlesbrough couldn't win owt. When we arrived at ten o'clock, the favourite occupation of the coaches was to sit on the radiators. If they were seeking inspiration, all they got were warm bums. 'OK, come on, let's go. Remember, it's ten, five and twelve' – same orders, same start to a session, day after day. It was an unnecessary reminder that we would be expected to run ten laps followed by five half-laps and twelve sprints. You did it in your own time and the lazy buggers would cut the corners and run on the grass. Only occasionally would they toss us a ball for a bit of a knockabout. How on earth could a training regime like that possibly help a group of blokes whose job demanded that they should manoeuvre a football better than the opposition, under the scrutiny of thousands of paying spectators, every Saturday afternoon? It struck me as barmy then, and any manager or coach who pays scant respect to the constant need for practice with a ball is barmy now.

It was Lindy Delapenha who eventually broke the monotony of it all by asking for volunteers to come back and play head-tennis in the afternoons. I was probably the first volunteer. We strung a rope from a drainpipe at the back of the stand to the fence of the factory next door – a span of about twelve yards. It was six a side with a shilling to the winners – 5p in today's money. They could play for five grand a man nowadays but it wouldn't be any more competitive than we were. In time, because it became the most popular part of training at Middlesbrough, we marked out the court with whitewash borrowed from the groundsman. Once the game was under way, you weren't allowed to let the ball touch the floor, and there were times when it would fly at you like a bullet. It didn't take a genius to work out that this was more closely related to the action of a Saturday afternoon than jogging and sprinting without a ball in sight.

For all the positive lessons I learned from Alan Brown, he had some peculiar training methods. At least we had a ball, and we wore our match strip and lined up as a team, but we played against nobody! Browny was a Lilleshall man – one of the managing and coaching fraternity who swore by the so-called education they gathered at that training establishment in Shropshire. It was regarded as a footballing university by the theorists, the fancy-dan coaches who had a thirst for what they called technical knowledge but who hadn't got the first idea about the way football really worked.

It was at Lilleshall that Bill Shankly, invited to give a talk I suppose, became so frustrated and angry about some demonstration they'd laid on that he left his seat, walked on to the pitch, grabbed the ball and half-volleyed it into one of the goals. 'That's better – it's safer in there,' he said, or words to that effect. Bill couldn't tolerate people who insisted on complicating the game. To him, that Lilleshall lot would have been talking in a foreign language.

Alan Brown believed and followed their theories. He became a fanatic about what he called shadow training – the first team against nobody. Word has it that after moving to Sheffield Wednesday he developed this form of practice match so that his team were confronted by eleven dustbins. At Sunderland we were confronted by nothing more threatening, challenging or realistic than an empty opposing half of the pitch. We played against invisible men and we usually won! Even though we did have a ball to work with, it was the most boring and meaningless activity I was ever involved in. I don't know whether it was intended to improve our understanding and vision, or whether it was just a matter of confidence in knowing that, eventually, we would have the satisfaction of putting the ball in the net. Whatever the intention, it was totally false, right down to Brown's instruction as he barked at us, 'Just do what you would do if there was an opponent standing in your way.'

'I would try to go round him and stick it in the net,' I told him many times. 'But there's nobody here. There's no bugger to go round so what do I do, just roll it in?'

'No,' Browny snapped, 'you smash it in.'

So I did. I finished up smashing them in from well outside the penalty area, from all parts and all angles, but I'll be blowed if I know what good it did because come Saturday Browny's theory went out of the window. Every time I looked up to take aim, or just hit the ball instinctively, there was some bloke, usually wearing a green jersey, hanging about between the posts trying to make bloody sure he kept it out. Shadow training? When did you last hear of shadows benefiting anybody's work – apart from the lads who backed Cliff Richard?

Working with the youngsters at Sunderland brought me into close contact with Colin Todd and John O'Hare, talented young men who were a pleasure to work with. Getting to know them as I did proved very useful when I came to sign them a little further down the line. The youngsters responded because my emphasis was on preparation for matches, working with an objective, a purpose, striving to make them as comfortable as possible with the ball. They would see little enough of it on a Saturday so it was common sense to make sure they had plenty of it during the week. It was during the matches, though, that they learned whether I was right or wrong in what I'd told them and asked them to do from Monday to Friday.

It's no good training to a peak if you reach that peak two days before the event. You don't have to be at your peak all the time to play well, either. I'd say there is a margin of roughly 15 per cent and a player can still perform well providing he doesn't drop any further than that.

A good coach or manager can't walk out there cold on a matchday; he has to be as worked up about the game as his players. You could call it fanaticism, and I know I had it. At the end of most matches as a manager, even as a coach with L plates at Sunderland, my shirt used to be as sweat-stained as any of the players'. Total involvement is what you must have. You must be on the same wavelength as the players, share their emotion whether that's elation or disappointment, and always believe you know why and where it has gone right or wrong.

After a few months, George Hardwick gave me a title, youth-team manager, and told me it would be to my benefit to take my coaching badge. It was on that FA course at Durham that I met Charlie Hughes who was to become top man in our game, Director of Coaching at FA headquarters. On the rare occasions that I can't get to sleep it's usually because somebody or something has reminded me that Charlie Hughes was on the short-list at the time I was interviewed for the England manager's job. What an insult! This was the man who argued that the quicker and more often you landed the ball in the opposing penalty area, the likelier you would be to score a goal. Some believed it. Some managers had their teams bouncing the ball off clouds to get it in the box, and their players piling in. I wonder what happened to the word 'creativity' in the Hughes approach.

You might argue with a certain justification that Wimbledon flourished from Charlie Hughes' football. Their rise from the bottom division to the top and their FA Cup win over Liverpool in 1988 – one of the biggest Wembley upsets of all time – was fairytale stuff. It was an extraordinary feat for them to make it to the old first division and to survive for so long in the Premiership, but there wasn't much sophistication about them. They pushed the rules to the limit and on too many occasions overstepped the mark. They were not an easy team to admire, compensating for lack of talent with an overuse of intimidation and brawn.

I'm sure that wasn't the kind of thing Hughes had in mind when he advised haste and distance in shifting the ball from A to B. Wimbledon took it to its extreme. Nevertheless, I don't think the man had any idea about the way in which football should be played. That's why I defied him at every twist and turn on that coaching course. I just had to tell him that, no, you didn't always have to head the ball with your forehead. You could stick it in with the side of your head or the back of it, your kneecap or your you know what, just so long as you stuck it in the net legally. Of course I was aware that the forehead is the largest part of the head. I didn't need him or anybody else to tell me that. It was all part of the theory and might have been accepted together with the rest of the bullshit by the accountants and clerks and other non-football blokes 'studying' with me at Durham. It didn't fool me and it didn't stop me from trying to prove Hughes wrong time and again. I kept telling the others in the group that there was an alternative to his way and they, like the youth players at Sunderland, listened to me.

That was further proof that I could get my point across. This was football, my subject, after all. I'd been a player and a good one; most of them hadn't. They were entitled to listen and I don't suppose any of them were surprised to learn that, despite Charlie Hughes, I qualified. I became one of the youngest in the country to get my full coaching badge. It didn't mean that much to me, bits of paper never have. On paper, Nottingham Forest shouldn't have been relegated. On paper, Wimbledon shouldn't have won the Cup. It's on the pitch that the truth comes out.

The truth was that I'd developed an instant liking for being in charge. The challenge of management was not just to my liking, it was one I knew I could meet and conquer. A coaching qualification hadn't proved anything like as much as the reaction of those young men at Roker Park, the ones who put into practice what I'd been telling them all week. They were the ones who convinced me I could be a manager. I was beginning to think I could be one of the best ever and it didn't take as long as I thought it would to prove it. George Hardwick lost his job at the end of the season and the bloke who took over, Ian McColl, did what most new managers do – he gathered his own staff around him.

My testimonial match at Roker Park did me two huge favours. A crowd of over 31,000 provided me with a windfall of approximately £10,000, and later, a word or two in the boardroom put me in the big time. Well, to a lad who had just had to finish as a youth-team manager, Hartlepools United *were* big time. Their chairman, a little bloke called Ernie Ord who turned out to be an absolute shit, offered me the job. Suddenly, I was the youngest manager in the Football League. The English game hadn't a clue about what was in store. The old fourth division had just been blessed with genius. I'm kidding, honest, but I'm not far wide of the mark.

I became the youngest manager in the League with exactly the right motivating forces in my head and in my heart. The chips on my shoulders were as hot as any you could find in a pan of boiling fat. I knew I should have had more recognition as a player. I was only really known and appreciated in Middlesbrough and Sunderland. England didn't seem to want a prolific goalscorer, and all those I scored for 'Boro had been wasted because of a rotten defence. It hadn't been my fault that they failed to get promotion to the top division. Then came the killer-blow – the injury. I could have disintegrated then. I was in my prime and anybody who could score twenty-eight goals in twenty-eight matches by the time Boxing Day came around – well, he couldn't have been far short of his peak, could he?

Beneath the brashness and conceit, and the feeling that I could be one of the best managers ever, there was fear as well – just a touch but enough to make sure I worked hard and took nothing for granted. It was the fear that had been instilled by my mam constantly reminding me that I didn't have a trade at my fingertips. All I had was a spell as head boy at school, eighteen months running messages at ICI, two years' national service with the RAF, and football. In other words, football was all I had. National service had taken two years out of a crucial stage of my life. I always envied lads who had a trade because some of them either avoided national service altogether or joined up at twenty-one once they had finished an apprenticeship. The difference between eighteen and twenty-one was massive, one a child, the other a man, with uncertain years in between. When that knee buckled underneath me, I could have been on the way to the scrapheap. That was when the fear crept in. Thank heavens for luck and for friends.

The legendary Len Shackleton is dead now, but never to be forgotten in my house, not only because of his dazzling talent with Sunderland and, staggeringly, only five times for England, but for the fact that he helped launch me into management. He'd had a word at Hartlepools, which was why they approached me on the night of my testimonial. Good old Len later had a word with the people who ran Derby County, easing my way in there, too. I had reasons to be thankful but those chips on my shoulder did my management prospects no harm at all. They taught me that I hadn't really appreciated what I'd got until it was denied to me, taken away completely.

You need friends in this life and I needed one in particular at Hartlepools. Peter Taylor had gone into management in his own right – ironically, with Burton Albion where our Nige has been cutting his teeth as a manager these past couple of years. He's doing extremely well so you never know, it might not be too long before another member of the Clough dynasty is continuing the tradition in the League.

A chuckle is the first thing that springs to mind whenever I think of Pete and that's the nicest legacy any man can leave. I've chuckled countless times at the recollection of our get-together in York. He'd have to take a cut in money to join me as assistant, of course he would, but I knew he was keen, if not desperate, to get into league football. I helped him make up his mind by giving him two hundred quid. I made many great signings in my time – Dave Mackay, Kenny Burns, Colin Todd, Peter Shilton, Garry Birtles, Roy McFarland, Trevor Francis, if I continued the list it would just about fill the rest of this book. But the best piece of recruitment I ever achieved was getting Peter Taylor, my mate and Uncle Pete to my kids, to join me in trying to make something out of a ramshackle, failing, totally skint football club called Hartlepools United.

Never was Pete's dry old sense of humour needed more than at Hartlepools. Never was his talent for spotting poor players and good replacements more of a priority. I can see him sitting there now, thinking, tongue in cheek, having slipped the *Sporting Life* from underneath his arm and flipped it on the table. 'Something's got to be done about this lot – and quick,' was his opening address. 'We're in the shit, good and proper. We'll be asking for re-election at the end of the season with this team. They're bound to finish bottom unless there's a place even lower in the bloody table.'

They had less than ten points and it was October. We were bottom of the entire Football League with defenders who couldn't defend, strikers who couldn't score, apart from a lad called Ernie Phythian who bagged a few, and the only thing the midfield could create was confusion among themselves. Our first thought was that they might respond to a bit of encouragement, but reality screamed at us that, overall, we'd been lumbered with a crap side. There were other important things to establish in those initial stages and I knew I would be at my strongest during the first three months. A manager always is – anybody starting a new job should make emphatic decisions in that time if they want to establish working conditions to suit them.

To my knowledge, Pete was the first number two in the game, or at least we were the first proper partnership. Chairman Ernie Ord and the directors needed convincing about Pete's role and seeing that we were going to have to do everything between us, including painting the stand and the barriers in the summer, Pete had to be the trainer as well. He was the bucket and sponge man on matchdays and there was nothing funnier than that. He knew nothing about joints, ligaments and tendons. If it couldn't be cured by sploshing a cold sponge on it and telling the injured player to 'gerrup and gerron wi' it', he had no cure at all, and I certainly didn't.

But we learned at Hartlepools. We learned how to ship out the deadwood and bring in better players. We learned how to lift a team from bottom in October to the safety of eighteenth place by the end of the season. We learned where to place buckets to catch the rain that leaked through the holes in the roof. We learned how to sign a youngster from grammar school whose head-master wanted him to go to university rather than to Hartlepools United, which wasn't an unreasonable point of view, I suppose. I persisted, arguing that surely the lad should have the choice, already knowing the boy wanted to sign for me.

So John McGovern became a professional footballer instead of a university student. He, Taylor and I were to have good reason to be thankful for the day he put pen to paper at the scruffy little club that gave us all a start. John McGovern of Nottingham Forest was to hold aloft the European Cup on all our behalves, not just once but in two consecutive seasons. Not many players, captains, have done that. People still ask me about the secrets of football management. How do you manage a football club? Read on . . .

C H A P T E R   3

GOALKEEPERS, CENTRE-HALVES AND CENTRE-FORWARDS

Len Shackleton left an entire page blank in his book, reserved for what he believed directors knew about football. If I'd had my way there would be a blank chapter in this book dedicated to the same subject. I have never understood why men with such poor knowledge, or no knowledge at all, insist they know about the game in general and the needs of management in particular.

The vast majority of them knew nothing in my days as a player, nothing in my time as a manager and the modern lot still know nothing today. Yet I continue to see them quoted in the newspapers and droning on in television interviews, trying to convince the public and themselves that they have the faintest idea of how football works. It makes my blood boil; it makes me want to put my foot through the television screen and

I'd have done it long before now but I have a dodgy knee to look after.

Football club chairmen and directors are still so barmy, so naïve, so thick and so stubborn yet full of themselves that they continue to make stupid decisions when it comes to the appointment of a manager. That is one of the reasons why there is such a turnover in my industry, so many sackings, resignations and departures explained by that cosy little phrase 'by mutual agreement', which I have never understood for the life of me. Many of the casualties are the victims not only of their own failure – they are the victims of chairmen and directors who shouldn't have given them the job in the first place.

Look at a couple of my former players, defender Colin Todd and Stuart Gray who used to do a job for me in midfield. Toddy, you won't need reminding, was a wonderful player, a brilliant defender who should have eased himself into the England side and stayed there for as long as he wanted. He did get twenty-seven caps, which is twenty-five more than I got, but there was a major difference between us. In my opinion, he didn't possess the same ambition I had to go along with his outstanding talent. I knew when I had Colin Todd playing for me at both Derby and Forest that it was highly unlikely he would make a top-notch manager.

I can sense it in people if I have enough regular contact. For instance, I always thought Martin O'Neill was cut out for a future in management because he was bright and sharp, a right smart-arse who was fully prepared to stand his ground and answer back when he believed he was right. He was also bursting with enthusiasm for the game.

It was not quite like that with Toddy. He managed Bolton for a while, twice relegated from the Premiership unless I'm wrong, so his track record wasn't that clever. Another example of a manager whose talent didn't meet the demands of the game at top level. Getting out of the first division is one thing but keeping a club in the Premiership asks even more of the man in charge. But in 2002, the directors of Derby, my club, decided in their wisdom that a change was needed and dear Jim Smith had to be replaced if the team was to survive among the top sides in the country. Todd was already at Pride Park and he was their man. They put him in charge. I could have told them they were taking a huge risk. Everything at a football club – success or failure, the sale of replica shirts, filling the executive boxes, and a million other things I could think of – is dependent on the performance of the man who creates and selects the team.

Do you think for a moment that Manchester United would have become the richest football club in the world without the expertise of Sir Alex Ferguson as manager? If you do, you're as daft as the directors who appoint managers who have no chance, absolutely no chance, of doing much apart from struggle. The Old Trafford empire, if that's what they call what is now one of the big financial institutions in our country, would not have developed the way it has without Fergie. Those who support United, those who direct it, those who buy shares in it and those who are paid such ridiculously high wages to play for it, they should all be eternally grateful to Sir Alex Ferguson and the ability he brought down from Scotland seventeen years ago.

It's not a coincidence that he has turned out to be United's most successful manager of all time, and I'm not underestimating what Sir Matt Busby did for them. Alex had done his time, served his apprenticeship, learned the ropes north of the border. He'd even known what it was like to get the sack before he emerged and blossomed with Aberdeen, and steered them to a European trophy. It hasn't been all plain sailing for him in Manchester, but his background means that at least the thinking in the United boardroom was sound. For once, directors, unless they've been extremely lucky, paid attention to the candidate's qualifications. Those who don't shouldn't be anywhere near a football club, but the game is littered with them.

I was at Pride Park in April 2002 and it was painful to watch my old team lose to Newcastle – a defeat that virtually sealed their relegation from the Premiership. They'd been two up with little more than a quarter of an hour to go – two up and they couldn't keep a clean sheet. That wasn't a mistake in my day – it was nothing short of a disgrace and a bloody crime. It was too late by the time John Gregory moved in from Villa, even though he won a game or two immediately after Toddy lost the job. Derby paid for bad judgement at boardroom level. You can't blame Colin for accepting the job;

I believe you must question the men who made the appointment.

Similarly, I wondered about Stuart Gray being given the manager's job at Southampton when Glenn Hoddle answered Tottenham's call 'home'. I'm not sure what job Gray had with the club, whether he was coaching the reserves or helping out with the first team. What I do know is I don't think it sufficient to qualify him for the job of manager of a team in the English Premiership. He couldn't have been right for it in normal circumstances because he had no experience to fall back on, but they weren't normal circumstances at Southampton – a club well acquainted with the struggle against relegation seeing that they've been involved in one for most of the seasons I can remember. Season 2001–02 was going to be one of the most important in the entire history of the club. They had left The Dell, their tight little ground that was worth several points a season to them because every other team hated playing there, and moved to a new home at St Mary's, one of those so-called state-of-the-art modern arenas. It was Mary, Mary, quite contrary as far as I was concerned when I heard young Gray had been made manager. It made no sense at all to me. He was a nice lad, I'm sure he still is, but wet behind the ears in management terms. Unless he was a genius so far undiscovered, he hadn't a prayer. If ever there was a season when survival in the Premiership was absolutely vital, that was it. Yet Southampton's directors, surely realising the team had lost the distinct advantage of playing home games at The Dell, chucked all that responsibility into the lap of an untried manager. He didn't last long. He couldn't last long, but when he made way for Gordon Strachan's return to management, why weren't serious questions asked of those who shoved Gray in at the deep end? Why weren't any of them held responsible? Why didn't any of them pay the price of losing his own position with the club? Why? Because they rarely do. Football chairmen and directors at any club you care to look at are among the great survivors in life.

Perhaps I was prejudiced against directors once I found myself working for that horrible little bugger Ernie Ord at Hartlepools. I suppose I do have to give him some credit for choosing me and hiring Peter Taylor as well. Hartlepools, a little club fighting for their existence at the wrong end of the entire League, was the ideal place for any ambitious young manager to learn to walk. Ernie Ord hadn't a clue what Pete and I were about, what we were doing on his behalf as the owner of the club. We not only won him a few matches and kept him in the League but we got his club in the newspapers on a regular basis, helped paint the ground and, all right, on occasions did threaten to sling him out physically.

Hartlepools suddenly found themselves getting more publicity, relatively, than some of the top clubs in the country – not as much as David Beckham's left foot when he injured it in the spring of 2002, but the game's even dafter now than it was then. Ord, having informed us that his son was going to deal with publicity all of a sudden, and having contemplated sacking Taylor, announced at a meeting of the directors that we had both been fired. Now there are two things you can do as a manager if you're sacked. You can go, hopefully with the necessary pay-off, or you can stay! At least you can if you're Clough and Taylor with the public support we had at a little club like Hartlepools almost forty years ago.

Ord couldn't have been the big man if he'd tried. As a bloke who was hardly tall enough to peer over the steering wheel of his Rolls-Royce, he was at something of a disadvantage. But like so many of his ilk, and so many in the game even now, he wanted to be seen as the man who ran the place and he wanted to be sure he took the credit. I spotted that early on and made sure the press were there when I learned to drive the team bus. It was made very clear to the supporters of Hartlepools that if this club was to go places, even by their modest standards, nobody would be left in any doubt about who was doing the steering.

Once he sold his drapery business Ord immersed himself in the club. I detested his interference, the way he insisted on knowing what Taylor and I were up to and he resented me telling him to keep his nose out. I was getting his little club in the papers so there was no need to have his son dealing with publicity. He was critical of Peter and we both felt he was trying to drive a wedge between us. He wanted the credit for the fact that all of a sudden his club was doing pretty well. I suppose it was Ord who made me wary of football club chairmen, right from the start.

It was no surprise that we saved them from the humiliation of finishing bottom and having to apply for re-election; no surprise, either, that we finished eighth from top in our second season. It wasn't my personal highlight of the year, though. That was the birth of our daughter Elizabeth, completing the threesome with Simon and Nigel. Married with three kids now – for me it was a big responsibility, those mouths to feed. I knew I could manage a football team. I knew I could be among the best in the business if somebody would give me the chance. I'm sure there are some today who believe they're entitled to their chance at a higher level, especially when they've put in their time lower down and achieved a level of success that should register in the boardrooms of bigger clubs.

The only thing I knew about Derby was that the town had a reputation in the locomotive industry and for building Rolls-Royces – aye, even though some of them ended up being driven by nasty little men like Ernie Ord. I also knew that Derby was one of the country's traditional football towns, steeped in the history of the game. The club was in the second division. It had been dozing for too long. It needed reawakening. Somebody had to set the alarm clock. When Taylor and I took over, the bells never stopped ringing.

Len Shackleton put us in for the job. Actually, Taylor and I had seen off the chairman at Hartlepools, somebody else had taken over from Ord, but Pete's feet had started to itch. He was convinced we'd done enough to earn our big break, and put Shackleton in the picture. It was Shack who arranged for me to meet Derby's chairman Sam Longson and I'd landed the job before I met the directors at the old Baseball Ground later that same week. I left Barbara and the two elder children in a nearby park and told her to expect me when she saw me. It might have been the quickest interview of all time until I told Longson and his cronies that I'd be bringing Peter Taylor with me. If they were hiring me, they were hiring him. We were a twosome, a partnership, a bit like Morecambe and Wise with me as the straight man. Yes, I know all about those who later enjoyed referring to us as the Kray twins!

My side of the meeting went swiftly and easily. 'My injury finished me as a player but gave me an early start to management at Hartlepools,' I told them. 'As you know, applying for re-election had become an annual event for them but we changed all that, left them in the top half of the division. We built them a new stand and we've left them solvent.'

Some words impress directors more than others. Solvent is one of them. At least, the Derby lot sat up and took notice at the mention of the word, and I can think of about forty clubs today the directors of which would be impressed by any prospective manager who used it. I had Derby's directors shuffling uneasily in their seats one minute and smiling the next when I told them, 'I cut the playing staff down. I got rid of the players who were crap and brought in one or two who were just a bit better.'

I told them I wanted their job even though I knew little about the place other than that Harry Storer had been their manager five years earlier. I told them if they had any doubts they should look at my record at Hartlepools. I knew I had caught them at their weakest moment because the team was having a bad time. They'd had to fire their manager Tim Ward and, most significantly of all, they were getting stick from the public. If there's one thing football directors cannot stand, it's the kind of criticism managers have to face on a regular basis. I knew I was on solid ground, not just because they needed help in their predicament but because Sam Longson had already promised me the job when I met him with Len Shackleton at Scotch Corner. By the time I rejoined Barbara and the kids in the park, Taylor's appointment had also been rubber-stamped. Those directors had just made the best decision they were ever likely to make but they hadn't a clue what they'd let themselves in for. There were to be some fantastic times to enjoy but there was also trouble ahead, trouble that would cost me the England manager's job, to name but one thing.

They made their decision for two main reasons – they'd had enough of Tim Ward and the crowd were spoiling their week. They worked in and around Derby and life was being made uncomfortable. Once directors feel uncomfortable, they shift responsibility to somebody else. I'm sure some of those on that Derby board must have gone home to their wives that day and said, 'We've got a right big mouth coming to work with us.'

Now those ladies wouldn't have known who the hell I was but after a couple of weeks they knew right enough because one of the first things I did was to introduce myself to all of them. They loved it. Within days, their enthusiasm had been rekindled to the stage where they were competing with one another for the prize of being in charge in the tearoom.

I didn't haggle over money. I didn't haggle with Longson at our original meeting and I didn't make an issue of it when I met his colleagues at the Baseball Ground. I settled for my £100 a week or whatever it was at the time. I told them I'd be buying a house and reminded them that they'd just hired a former centre-forward who had more than 30,000 people turn up at his testimonial, just in case they weren't aware of how good a player I'd been.

Once the meeting was formally closed I told them, 'Right, now we can talk football. I don't know what's been going on at this club but I do know that you've got a part-timer playing for you and that's no bloody good to me for a start.'

'What do you mean, part-timer?'

'Ian Buxton, your centre-forward.' You have to spell it out for people like them. 'The lad who plays cricket for Derbyshire and is given time off and doesn't join up with us until September. I can understand him needing the break but by the time he's available to me, your team could be at the arse-end of the second division.' They looked aghast – the perfect situation for me to press my point. 'I love cricket but I love this job even more at the moment, and I'm telling you that if Buxton doesn't turn up for pre-season training, he doesn't play for me.'

'But he has an agreement in writing,' one of them protested. He had – their blessing for a two-week holiday after finishing with his cricket.

'Good for him,' I told them. 'I'm sure it's a beneficial agreement from Ian's point of view but if you've got twenty players on your books at Derby, I'm down to nineteen before I've even arrived.' I could sense that uneasy shifting and shuffling of backsides around the boardroom table. Perfect. 'It's not on. It's no good to me. I'm rescinding that agreement here and now and I don't care whether it's in writing or not – on headed notepaper or daubed all over the dressing room wall.'

Mission accomplished, first job done. I didn't know whether they were going to like me. I didn't know if they would always support me although the likelihood was that they wouldn't. But what I did know as I walked out of the ground and went to rejoin Barbara and the kids was that those directors knew exactly who would be running their club. If they were uncomfortable and longing to shift responsibility, they'd picked the right man. Needless to say, one of the first tasks Taylor and I carried out was transferring Ian Buxton to Luton. He wasn't a bad player but he would have been a non-playing centre-forward for at least two weeks and I think that's crackers.

Centre-forwards, centre-halves, goalkeepers, in that order or in reverse order – you've heard me mention them umpteen times and the system applied at Derby as much as anywhere else in football in England, Brazil or Outer Mongolia. That was the system we used from the very beginning at Derby. On Taylor's recommendation, or instruction, I returned to Sunderland and signed John O'Hare for £21,000, so Buxton was replaced by a young man with tremendous ability.

We persevered with the goalkeeper for some time because, even in his late thirties, Reg Matthews was 'the bravest player on the staff', according to Peter Taylor. Eventually, though, he had to go and Pete brought in his man, Les Green from Burton Albion. The centre-half, Bobby Saxton, had shot it and his replacement became key to just about everything we were to achieve with Derby. Everybody knows about our late arrival at Roy McFarland's front door on Merseyside and us asking his dad to get him out of bed. Some managers might have agreed to Roy's request to sleep on the prospect of a move from Tranmere to Derby but some managers don't have any idea. I knew Liverpool or Everton or some other club would sign him if we didn't – he had so much potential. It must have been gone midnight but the instinct was still sharp. I had to clinch it somehow. I told him Taylor and I were going to turn Derby into one of the best teams in the country and that if he insisted on sleeping on it I'd still be there in the morning, offering him the chance to be a part of something big. He signed and went on to become the best centre-half to play for England for many a year, arguably the best ever.

People began to sit up and take notice of Derby County despite the fact that we were crap in that first season, conceding seventy-eight goals, seven more than we scored, and finishing in eighteenth place. The changes had been gradual, John McGovern arriving from Hartlepools, Alan Hinton switching from Nottingham Forest's left-wing to Derby's and the introduction of other new faces. In fact, we changed almost the entire side apart from the good players already on the books -- Kevin Hector up front, Alan Durban in midfield and Ron Webster at the back.

Taylor and I were in our element. We were never more excited or effective than when we were building teams from basics, getting rid of the dead wood and planting fresh new saplings. I was talking a lot, making the back pages a lot, attracting journalists like flies. Suddenly Derby were news again. A pressman loves nothing more than knowing that when he takes the trouble to go to see a manager, he'll come away with a worthwhile piece to write. When they came to see me, they usually left with enough copy to keep them going for a week. I had been used to publicity throughout my playing career because I scored goals and goalscorers are guaranteed a mention. I wanted publicity at Hartlepools because it served my purpose -- it reminded people that the town still had a football club.

I think those Derby directors had a few doubts in that first season when we finished lower than Tim Ward had managed the season before, but they changed their tune a year later. They were all there to be seen in the front row of the stand, no longer uncomfortable, no longer worried about the crowd on their backs. They wanted the lot. They were revelling in it, lapping it up. That's how directors re-emerge when the good times come to call, and for those at Derby there had never been a day like the one when we celebrated winning the second division championship.

Clough and Taylor had arrived on the scene and shaken a few egos in the process. We had transformed an ordinary, small-town club in the space of two seasons and there were many, no doubt, who believed it had been done as much by luck as by judgement. I don't think they were saying the same thing three years later when we won the league title. True to form, I was sitting on the beach in the Scilly Isles the day the championship was confirmed, relaxing in the grand manner, having no doubt been for a nice long walk on the water.

How did it happen, why did it happen, what is a good manager or management partnership and how do they pull it off? How *do* you manage a football club successfully? I will get round to explaining, honest. It's the most common and fiercely burning question in football because good managers, great managers, are like the best diamonds – rare and priceless. All I can tell you is how I did it, how Clough and Taylor did it.

HOW TO MANAGE A FOOTBALL CLUB

What I'm about to say should interest all managers and would-be managers, all those who think they can do the job and all those who might be planning to have a crack at it in the future. Coaches in particular, those people who prefer to be called a coach rather than a manager, might just learn something.

Some will appreciate the value of what they're about to read, others will say I'm stating the obvious and that the job can't possibly be as simple as I make it out to be. Those who can't see the point in what I say and those who continue to insist that football is far more intricate and complicated, technical and sophisticated – whatever phrase or description they prefer to justify their own opinion – well, they are too thick to become good managers anyway.

Talking came naturally to me, even though I was a

late starter. I was around five before I could string plenty of words together. I had no trouble talking to schoolteachers, headmasters, other parents and their bairns. I had no trouble talking to the policeman or the bloke who used to come to Valley Road selling his herrings. I had no problem facing microphones or television cameras. I opened the first sports programme they had on Tyne Tees Television and I also presented a programme for the BBC. I was pleased but not surprised when I discovered that football management also came naturally to me.

If you could wander into a public library and pick up a foolproof guide on how to manage a football team, everybody would be able to do it. But you can't. That's why I'm considering opening the Brian Clough Academy of Management – only kidding, but it couldn't fail. They'd be queuing overnight, those budding bosses and all the failures and even some of those who think they can do it already. Kevin Keegan might just learn something about how to get the best out of the best players in the country. I never had the opportunity but I think I might have done it just a shade better than he did.

I used to play at centre-forward, as you might have gathered (267 goals in 296 appearances for Middlesbrough and Sunderland – go on, digest the figures again). I knew that goals won matches, which told me, as a manager, that I needed somebody who could score them. Then I thought, 'Who is the one who stops the other team from scoring?' The centre-half – two centre-halves these days but the principle is the same. Any team of mine would need a good centre-forward and a good centre-half. In our time together at Middlesbrough, with a first-team defence leaking like a rusted bucket, Taylor convinced me about the true value of the goalkeeper; hardly surprising, seeing that's where he played.

'No point in you scoring three if our bloke's letting three in,' he'd keep saying, time after time, day after day. 'There are key positions in any side where real talent is vital. If necessary, you can fill-in everywhere else.'

So I signed good goalkeepers. In fact, I've never fathomed why top keepers don't cost as much as top strikers. A save can be as important as a goal but a mistake by a keeper is often more costly than a miss by his team-mate at the opposite end of the field.

One of my earliest worries at Derby concerned the keeper. As I mentioned, Reg Matthews was getting on in years and I was convinced he was well past his best. He was good enough to play for England on five occasions but it had been ten years since his last cap. Taylor insisted that 'Matthews might have "shot it" but he's the bravest player on the staff.'

That immediately attracted me to him and convinced me I should persevere with him for a while. No matter how good you are as a footballer, if you're frightened it is a big minus, a big handicap. There are many players who can get away with a certain lack of ability because they are particularly courageous. Very few, if any, can get away with not being brave at all, however talented they might be. Ability will never blossom if a lad is too frightened to have the ball.

To have possession of a football generates a kind of fear in itself, an apprehension, concern about being able to control it and find a team-mate when you decide to let it go. But physical fear is a player's worst enemy. Some players used to study match programmes to see if an opponent they'd faced before was playing. If the programme was available on a Friday night, they'd look at it then. If not, it would be on matchday. If a player's thinking, 'Bugger me, that's the same fella who kicked me last season and I can still feel it,' he's going to be second-best before the teams reach the pitch so there's no earthly point in sending him out in the first place.

So Reg Matthews's courage kept him in my Derby side for a while, despite the fact that he couldn't always get to the shots that were flashed at him because the old reflexes had gone a bit; either that or, as a heavy smoker, his eyes were still watering from the fags he'd had before the game.

I tried to make sure of one basic thing in management. Educated people would call it a fundamental but I'm not sure what that means. I know what basic means and my basic was that there should never ever be the slightest sense of complication in my dressing room. Footballers, by and large, are not academics. They are people who realise from an early age that, with any luck, they will be playing for their livings. I'm not saying they all abandon their education but I know from my own experience that once I realised I was a bit special at football, geography and history never grabbed my attention anywhere near as much as the games lessons!

I would far rather have my players rolling about the dressing room floor laughing than have them trying to fathom a list of instructions and tactics before they went out to play a match. In fact, Taylor had them laughing like that on countless occasions, in training, on the coach, around the ground and on matchdays.

Discipline was crucial. Without discipline you have no team, or at least you don't have a team that will do itself full justice and operate to its full potential. I could never have players who set out, or were even prepared, to make life more difficult than it already was for referees and their linesmen. I couldn't abide players being late for training. Alan Brown, I'm certain, would have liked nothing more than to fine me for turning up late at Sunderland. He'd glance at his watch every single morning but he never caught me out and my money was safe in my pocket.

Discipline was no great issue, no big deal, at Derby or at Forest later on. It was routine. They knew that I would be the same bloke every day – awkward, inevitably bad-tempered and for ever talking, reminding them that this was the good life. Playing for your living, being able to look forward to your work every day, was a great privilege afforded to very few people. I suppose it was only when we'd won or when the close season arrived that I was totally relaxed and liveable with.

One of the first things I'd hear when I arrived at the ground in the morning would be somebody whispering, 'I wonder what kind of mood he's in?' The moment I heard it I'd shout, 'I'm in a rotten mood. Start off believing that and you won't go wrong. Believe I'm in a rotten mood every time you see me and you'll be fine. On that basis, I can only get better.'

Yes, of course we had a laugh as well. That was just as important – part and parcel of the variety required to relax those involved in a high-tension industry. I'm not sure how often top footballers laugh today but I don't see many smiles on the pitch or in front of the television cameras afterwards. Priorities seem to have gone wrong with the modern bunch – over the edge in the sense that everything they do, every aspect of the game that makes the papers, is dominated by the mention of money. Players have always wanted to be paid well; it was no different in my day although we were never paid well at all. It was right that footballers should be awarded salaries in keeping with their value as entertainers, packing the stadiums and generating so much wealth for their employers, but money has become something of an obsession. I get the impression, looking at some of them, that all they do every day is go home and count their cash. Security is a wonderful thing in anybody's life. Today's footballers are financially secure virtually from the moment they make the first team. There's not a lot wrong with that but I'm sure that, like me, the general public must be sick and tired of hearing how rich they are.

People continue to wonder whether I would have been as successful as a manager in today's climate of multi-millionaire players and their interfering agents. Well, whatever the money and the drastic shift in the balance of power, it would have made no difference to me whatsoever. There is no doubt that players have become more powerful than they were, more independent, more capable of calling the shots if weak managers allow them to. That's what money does. But the principles of management remain the same. Ground rules apply just as much to millionaires as to those who can hardly afford to pay the mortgage. I applied them from the start, telling my players exactly what was expected and what would happen if those rules were broken, and I always ended by asking, 'Have you heard everything I've said?'

It usually met with the stock reply, 'Yeah, yeah, Gaffer. We've heard it that many times we know it off by heart.'

'Right, then,' I said. 'And do you agree? Is there anybody who wants to say anything? If you all agree to a fifty-pound fine if you're late, then that's the rule. No point in cribbing when I demand the fifty quid.'

Somebody would say something like, 'But what happens if we get caught in heavy traffic on the way or we're involved in an accident?'

'An accident, that's different. That's exceptional. But busy roads? Don't give me that. We all have to contend with traffic and if it's that bad where you live, set off a bit earlier. What do you want – a ten o'clock start for training or ten thirty? And don't tell me ten thirty would have your missus complaining it made you late for lunch. It's up to you.' It usually became ten thirty on a majority vote. That became the rule and they'd laid it down themselves.

I wasn't programming my players or turning them into robots in any shape or form. I was simplifying their lives, spelling out with their agreement what would happen in a given set of circumstances – lateness for instance, failure to dress properly when required, getting booked for things that could be avoided such as kicking the ball away in disgust or anger and mouthing off at a referee or a linesman. It was easy enough to get booked anyway, and it's a darned sight easier in today's football, so what was the point in adding to the risk of suspension just because you couldn't control your temper? I saw many things in my time as a manager, many changes along the way. What I didn't see was a referee change his mind and his decision after a player either effed and blinded at him or whacked the ball into the back row of the stand.

I wasn't being heavy handed or dictatorial although, yes, I was a bit of a dictator in my time. Had to be. But in laying down the rules with them, I always had their interests at heart because whatever else I might be, I'm a players' man. After all, they're the ones who win matches for you. On the other hand, they won't win as many as they should if half of them are getting themselves banned through their own stupid irresponsibility.

Little things mean a lot in management. Take

Fridays at Nottingham Forest when we were playing away next day. Inevitably, we had to travel on Friday nights. You couldn't risk going reasonable distances on Saturday morning because of the traffic. For another thing, a long coach journey on the day of the game isn't conducive to fitness and the right frame of mind.

'So we'll all come in at three o'clock Friday afternoon and do some training,' I told them at Forest. I'm sure I did something similar at Derby because that was the way I worked. 'And when you come in, make sure you're ready to leave. Have your smart gear for travelling. You know the drill. We'll train, have a bath and I'll get a meal laid on for us at the restaurant up the road.'

Common sense told me that if you travelled at five o'clock on a Friday afternoon, you'd cop for all the traffic. We'd leave the restaurant at half past six or so. Then it was on the coach, game of cards, in London or wherever we were going by half past eight. By the time we'd checked in, found our rooms, come down, read a paper, it was time for bed and 'See you all at eleven o'clock in the morning.' They loved it. It saved their wives cooking for a start, and they knew I'd have everybody back home by half past eight on the Saturday night. We might have Sunday, Monday and sometimes even Tuesday off as well.

Do you know why they loved it? It was because I was doing the thinking for them. It suited them not to have too many decisions to make. Some players don't like making decisions and when I made them, I did it in the interests of their families as well. It suited the wives because they were not being messed about with silly times. It suited the bairns because they were seeing plenty of their fathers rather than an hour here and half an hour there. The players had the opportunity to stay in bed if they wanted – Archie Gemmill, for example, would go to bed on Sunday and stay there all day. He'd get up for a meal and then go back. Those days off, sometimes three in a row, were good thinking on my part because it was like a holiday, and when the players came back to work, they wanted to be there – either to escape from the wife and kids or to avoid the washing-up.

It wasn't the same on the pitch. You still have some thinking to do with a ball at your feet. It's the feet that hold the key. If you can control a ball, you are three-quarters of the way there. With most footballers, it's a natural thing and it reduces some of the need to think on the field.

I was for ever reminding them how much I sweated on matchdays, like them. 'But do you have to shout all the time?' they'd protest every now and then. They always received the same reply. Yes, I did have to shout – not all the time but most of the time. I'd shout reminders, adjustments when they occasionally got themselves out of position, which is easy to do in the heat of the moment. I'd emphasise the need to keep the ball and to pass it forward whenever possible. I had to shout to tell them they weren't tired when sometimes they thought they were. Contact was vital because it made me one of them, part of the team. It was the same with discipline and those all-important rules. Footballers are normal people with normal emotions and they need a bit of help and reassurance from time to time. They need to feel a sense of familiarity and comfort in what they are being asked to do. Being high-profile doesn't make them any less normal than a bricklayer on a building site. It just makes them richer. If ever any of them showed signs of getting carried away, I saw it as my job to keep his feet on the ground. They were never in any doubt about who was boss because I told them myself – 'There's nothing the matter with a place being run by a dictator – as long as that dictator is me.'

It's a good job talking came easily to me because talking is a major aspect of the job. I don't care if you're a manager, a coach, a university lecturer, an orchestra conductor or the bloke who sold his herrings in Valley Road – if you can't get your message across, you might as well pack in and do something else. When my players reported back for a new season, they heard a familiar theme: 'It's now July and we're working again. Two plus two equals four and, come next April, it will still equal four. Nothing will have changed that drastically and nothing is going to change drastically with your game, either. We hope you've all got a bit richer, we hope you're more content, we hope you're more mature and we hope you won't run foul of the rules we've laid down. It's going to be a tight ship because, as you well know, that's the way I believe it should be done.' And they'd take my word for it.

I took charge of pre-season training because I believed it to be so important. It's like taking the first steps on a long military campaign. Make sure you've got your helmet on securely in July and it will keep you safe right the way through.

A team that has sound discipline will always have a greater chance than one whose players don't know how to behave in a decent manner. Pre-season was the time to remind my lot, 'Do things properly and we might all achieve what we have in common, the desire to succeed. We all want to be able to look back, have a medal to show to our kids, raise our standard of living and pay off the mortgage. We want to finish in May and say it's all been worthwhile. And during our break next summer, we want to be sitting on a beach or climbing a mountain, maybe riding a bike, with satisfaction and pride in what we've achieved. Believe me, you'll feel in better nick if you've achieved something that makes you proud. There is no greater satisfaction in life than doing your job well. If we all do that, everybody benefits.'

As far as timekeeping was concerned, I'd tell them, 'I started at twelve minutes past seven when I had to work for a living as a messenger boy. Don't ask me why it was twelve minutes past but it was. It meant me getting up at six in the morning and riding five or six miles on my bike whether the sun was shining or it was snowing or pissing down, all for a couple of quid a week. You lot don't have to be in until half past ten. You've got swanky cars and nice houses. You can get up, have a bite of breakfast while watching TV, read the paper and come in to a very pleasant working environment. You don't have to go down a coalmine and work in the dark for eight hours and you don't have to put up with a lot of noise apart from the occasional shout from me.

'You've got yourselves a good job. Don't you dare dissipate the advantages and privileges a good job gives you. If you can't get into work by half past ten in the morning, you're not worth bothering about and I certainly won't waste my time on you. It is natural for a man to come into work, it's not natural for him to want to sit in a chair all day long – there are enough of them having to do that through no choice of their own.

'Go down to the local infirmary and have a look in Ward 7 and then try feeling sorry for yourself and telling me you've got a rotten job. Go and hang the washing out for the entire family by nine o'clock in the morning like my mam had to do.'

The rules are the rules. We all have to abide by them, on and off the field, because somebody has written them down. They might be good or they might be bad but the rules enable us to have a game. Without them, there is no game at all. Everybody makes mistakes. I haven't seen a goalkeeper yet who hasn't let a ball slip through his hands when he should have stopped it with his eyes closed. I've never seen a centre-forward who hasn't missed a simple chance to score. I've never seen a perfect referee, either. In fact, I've not seen a perfect anything in life (apart from me!). My players learned to understand that referees were doing their best, honestly and in keeping with whatever talent they had for the job. It developed into a kind of mutual respect for one another – my lot made life as comfortable as possible for match officials, and they were quick to appreciate it. I lost count of the number of referees who came to me both at Derby and Forest and said, 'I'd just like to express my thanks. I love matches involving your team. We never have any trouble with them.'

It worked to our benefit. A team of mine was the referees' best friend. It was only human nature that they should have a sympathetic outlook towards us. They wouldn't bend the rules or do us any particular favours but they knew that my players were not cheating or taking liberties. A mistimed tackle was exactly that and nothing more sinister. When a player of mine stayed down with an injury, no one was in the slightest doubt that he was genuinely hurt.

I made a point of going to talk to referees at their meetings. Inevitably, I was asked about the badly behaved sides and I told them, 'That problem could be eliminated overnight. If a team persistently has players in trouble, especially for dissent, arguing and cussing and swearing, they should fine the managers concerned – a month's wages. If a manager was hit in his pocket, he'd be quick to get rid of the rotten apples in his barrel. He wouldn't stand for some yob or thug costing him his wages.'

I think Arsene Wenger should have been fined several times for his team's behaviour – forty-odd sendings off in his first five years as manager is nothing short of a disgrace. I don't care how successful he's been, how many trophies Arsenal have won – the shine on those trophies has been tarnished as far as I'm concerned because they have been won by an extremely talented team who have devalued their own achievements by often behaving like brats. No, Arsenal have not been a dirty team but they have been a bad-tempered, bad-mannered team and as far as I can see Wenger has either done little to change it or has failed to have much of an impact.

He comes across on television as a polite, charming, kind, intelligent man with an accent we all fall for. He speaks English better than they do in Hartlepool. Then we analyse the situation. He's with one of the biggest clubs in the country but he cannot justify the number of players Arsenal have had booked and sent off. I think it's no good him (like so many managers) saying he didn't see the incident in question because if his eyesight is as bad as it seems to be when an Arsenal player lands in trouble, he couldn't be the talented manager he is.

I've heard and read so much rubbish over recent seasons with players, managers, so-called television and radio experts complaining about bad refereeing. I can't believe they stop to think about the reality of the situation before they open their mouths. Referees are no worse than they ever were. The chances are that they're even a wee bit better. Their problem lies with players who make their lives a misery, kidding about injuries, diving for free-kicks and penalties, trying to get opponents booked or sent off, arguing with linesmen as if the award of a throw-in is as important to them as the size of their wage packet. Referees are being conned right, left and centre and then taken to task by people in a television studio with every electronic gadget technology can produce. The referee has no chance. Of course he makes errors of judgement but not as many as the player who is only too eager to chase him half the length of the field to tell him that he's dropped a clanger.

Scrutiny is the referees' greatest enemy. Their performance is watched and recorded from just about every imaginable angle. Eventually, after as many re-runs of the slow-motion replay as it takes, the experts make up their minds and declare whether the referee was right or wrong. Would you like to have your every move at work recorded and analysed by some smart-arsed expert who hasn't a clue what it's like to do your job in the first place? Of course you wouldn't and neither would I. The only thing that surprises me about modern refereeing is that so many people volunteer to do it.

I was lucky in being allowed to run the show. There's no doubt about it, in the early stages at Derby and nearly all the time at Forest I ran the show lock, stock and barrel. I had some players with strong personalities over the years, including Dave Mackay, Kenny Burns and Larry Lloyd to name just three, but they all toed the line. I didn't need to tell them I ran the place – they could see it. I think players need that; they prefer to know who is boss, how far they can go in a given situation and where angels fear to tread. I suppose, with me, they were never quite sure. Oh they were well aware that they had to stay within the rules, but they could never be certain how I was going to react from one day to another. They knew I would be striving to help them be part of an extremely successful team – what they didn't know was exactly how I would go about it, how today might differ from yesterday. Uncertainty is a good thing if you apply it properly.

What I set out to do – and this was a natural thing, an instinct rather than a planned philosophy – was to embrace the particular strengths of my players. Kenny Burns joined me with a reputation for being a dirty so-and-so as well as having a lifestyle that, well, let's say didn't portray him as a model professional. Reputations can be misleading. He turned out to be as nice a lad as I have ever managed – the opposite of his image. No, I'm not forgetting that he was a fierce competitor on the field, a tough Scot capable of cutting you in two. He deserved his medals, including the European Cup, and he deserved his honour as Footballer of the Year.

Lloyd was Lloyd. Some people thought Pete Taylor and I were barmy when we signed him but Taylor particularly knew he had what we required from a centre-half. Larry was a big lad. When he finished playing he went into the licensed trade and became the only landlord I knew who was bigger and wider than his own pub. I think his size, well over six feet, gave him a feeling of grandeur. We knew that he could give our team a sense of stability providing we restricted him to the simple things he could do well, and jumped on him if he attempted anything that was beyond his capability.

Dave Mackay was the total professional from start to finish. He was set to leave Tottenham, where he won the double, and go back to Edinburgh to become assistant manager of Hearts. Bill Nicholson, the Spurs manager, made it clear to me when I turned up in London that I had no chance of signing him for Derby, but I had to have a crack at it. I was in awe of Bill Nicholson because he was one of the game's legendary figures, a great manager and a great man. But if you are to have the slightest chance of succeeding as a football manager, you have to pursue your instincts and your judgement all the way. Bill was a bit dismissive on my arrival at White Hart Lane. Sign Dave Mackay? I got the impression I'd be better off turning round and driving back to Derby.

Mackay himself was just as dismissive. He was going to Hearts to be an assistant manager, no arguing, no move to Derby, no chance. Forget it. This was Dave Mackay I was talking to, one of the real greats as far as I was concerned. Taylor and I had agreed that he was just the man we needed to complete our team at Derby, to turn it into one with the potential to be really outstanding. I had to talk this man into joining a team he knew next to nothing about. So I talked. You can't teach that kind of thing at any academy or on any coaching course. I talked about wanting to build a team that would beat every other. I talked about how I wanted that team to play. I talked about generalities and specifics and soon I had him talking as well.

Timing is as important in negotiations as it is with a ball at your feet. Bang! 'What would it take to get you to Derby?' I hit him with the question the moment his dismissive mood seemed to mellow just slightly. When he said he'd consider £15,000 I said I couldn't raise that much and he said he'd be on his way to Hearts then. 'I think I can raise fourteen thousand,' I said, instinct again. Mackay didn't hesitate – 'Done.'

It had taken a good couple of hours at White Hart Lane to sign the player I had no chance of signing. He was going to transform my team and I was going to give Dave Mackay his second lease of life. He was disappearing from the English game but I brought him back from the brink to discover that, given the right setting and the right players around him, he could still win championships. He was on borrowed time with fourteen grand spread over three years. I never did a better piece of business in my entire career although the man himself had serious doubts the minute he arrived at the Baseball Ground.

It had been Taylor's original idea that we try to sign him, Taylor at his very best, doing what nobody ever did better – assessing a team, deciding what it needed most of all and knowing precisely the best man to provide that key element. It was Pete's suggestion – my job to do the rest. That was the way it worked with the Clough-and-Taylor partnership. And when it came to convincing somebody he could do something he'd never even considered, we had a technique.

'Better get him in here so you can talk to him,' Taylor told me next day when Mackay arrived to complete his move. 'Er, Dave, I think you'd better listen to what the Gaffer's got to say. He's got a new job for you.' Mackay's eyes switched from Taylor on one side of him to me on the other, and they kept switching their line of vision like a spectator at Wimbledon's Centre Court as we employed the technique that became our speciality.

'We're going to play you as a sweeper.' He protested, of course. He wasn't a sweeper, never had been, never would be, never could.

'I've covered every blade of grass on every pitch I've ever played on,' he said. 'That's my game, that's my style. I can't play as a sweeper.'

I told him he could and that once he'd seen our centre-half Roy McFarland (nineteen years old) and full-backs John Robson (eighteen) and Ronnie Webster who was still a young man but hadn't fulfilled his potential or ambition, he'd know he could. I surrounded Dave Mackay with young talent who would do the running and the donkey work and allow him not only to give our team the perfect finishing touch but to make them better players in the process. I said a few pages ago that I'd never seen anything that was perfect – Dave Mackay playing in that Derby defence was as near to perfection as makes no difference.

People who can't manage a football team would never have seen the reason to change the role of a man like Dave Mackay. Coaches who might have thought of it in the back of their cluttered and complicated minds wouldn't have had the guts or the way with words to put it across to the man himself and get him to agree. Taylor's idea, my persuasion – once it was put into practice it all made perfect sense. Not a lot alters in football when you think about it, apart from the number of noughts on the players' wage slips. The dimensions of the pitch remain virtually the same and the goalposts are where they've always been, even though some strikers still have a lot of trouble hitting the target that's never been known to move.

The skill of good management lies in assessment, judgement and motivation. It lies in knowing what your team needs, recognising the player or players capable of providing it and making bloody sure that every single one of them in your dressing room gives absolutely everything, match in match out, in the interests of the team. Defenders defend, midfield players provide the link and create and, if you're lucky, strikers score goals. It never ceases to amaze me that so many people have so much difficulty in assembling a good football team. How can they make such a simple job so complex?

C H A P T E R 5

TWENTY YEARS AHEAD OF OUR TIME

You can't buy a manual on management and sorry to all those who think you can learn how to be a manager simply by copying the exploits of others. Nobody can do the job in precisely the same way as someone else. But anybody who wants to know about management at its best, the effects of a partnership working in perfect harmony, should make a close study of what happened at Derby County from the moment Peter Taylor and I arrived in the summer of '67 to the time we stupidly walked away from it all in the autumn of '73. That period in Derby's history, and in my career, was the definitive example of football management in all its aspects and all its glory.

Taylor and I built two teams in that short time. The Mackay side won the second division championship, and we reshaped, refined and improved it so thoroughly and effectively that we won the league title three years later.

In many ways, football management is an instinctive process. I was blessed with an assistant of Peter Taylor's calibre, providing the elements of the job that I didn't have. In fact, Peter was in his element at Derby, coming up with the right names at the right time – as I've said, he told me to go and sign Mackay, believing in his own mind that I had no chance of pulling it off.

I can't overstate the impact and influence Mackay had at the Baseball Ground. Our self-belief – mine, Taylor's and the entire team's – stemmed from the confidence of Mackay himself. It won him the Footballer of the Year award and it won us that second division title. Mackay taught my two boys, Simon and Nigel, how to kick a football. He would spend hours on end with them, practising in what we called our shooting-box – a little wooden target area under the main stand at the Baseball Ground. It was sad when his playing days ended. He was what I had always believed him to be before I knew him and came to admire him so much – a man of immense talent, hard as nails on the pitch but with a gentle and pleasant nature off it, the consummate, complete professional. It was Dave Mackay who not only took over from Taylor and me, but led Derby to another league championship in 1975.

When Mackay stopped playing, we were faced with the problem of replacing him. How do you replace a legend? But we were full of ourselves in those wonderful days at Derby. Others would have been daunted by the prospect but we knew exactly how to go about it, who to get. 'You know everything there is to know about Colin Todd so you'd better get up to Sunderland and sign him,' was Taylor's solution, and no sooner said than done, as usual. The chairman? I never felt the need to ask Sam Longson. It never dawned on me because I was running the club. I felt totally in charge and success or failure was down to me. I was happy to have the buck firmly in my grasp.

Toddy cost us £175,000 which was an absolute fortune in those days – and far too much in the eyes of men who didn't understand management and never would. Longson was probably telling the story until the day he died – how that young bugger Clough took it upon himself to go and sign Colin Todd without a word until he sent a telegram to say he'd done it and that he'd virtually bankrupted the club. It wasn't big-headedness on my part although, aye, it was a wee bit cheeky. I saw it as my job to sign the best talent. Our judgement had been proved to directors who couldn't tell a good player from a bad player in any case, and as far as the money was concerned I knew we could afford it, if only just.

Few managers enjoyed that kind of freedom; even fewer would be given such privilege these days. But that was management as I saw it and, after all, few were as good as I was at the time. Nobody was as good as Taylor.

Many clubs had watched Archie Gemmill, the little Scotsman who was running Preston's midfield. Many scouts and managers had watched him several times but

Taylor needed no further confirmation once he'd cast that expert eye of his. Gemmill was the one, Gemmill had to be signed. Get off your arse and get it done, which I did, even though the awkward little sod said he wouldn't sign. He insisted on thinking about it over-night, unlike Roy McFarland earlier. I'm always amazed when managers allow players to go away and consider a proposed transfer. Let them out of your sight or your grasp and the chances are they'll sign for somebody else, especially nowadays with an agent on the other end of a mobile phone telling him he can always get him a better deal. If Gemmill was going to sleep on it, I was going to sleep alongside him, or at least in the spare bedroom. Funny, looking back – his wife Betty was pregnant with Scot who was later to play not only for my Nottingham Forest side but for Scotland as well.

After a hearty breakfast and helping with the washing-up, I signed Archie Gemmill. Once again, he was among the finest of our signings. Of all the foot-ballers who have played for me, including Martin O'Neill, Gemmill was one whom I believed would turn out to be a successful manager. He was to play or work for me until I packed in as a manager and his knowledge of the game is second to none. He had a crack at management but it didn't work out and I can only assume it was a problem of personality rather than ability. He was always a bit dour, miserable-looking. It must have given a wrong impression because Archie had what it takes to be in charge of a football team.

It is no exaggeration when I talk of Taylor and me

being twenty years ahead of everybody. We were fortunate to have the ability to recognise who could play and who couldn't. You'd be amazed at how many people who earn their money in football don't know that. It's the secret behind everything. Peter could spot them, I could sign them, and I knew how to handle the lot of them. I didn't recognise danger. I was like the twenty-year-old pilot in the war who went up in a Spitfire to take on half a dozen German fighter planes. I didn't know the meaning of fear. I thought I could shoot down the lot. I had age on my side and that was a big advantage. You don't see the possible pitfalls when you're thirty. When you get into your fifties and sixties, you see nothing else.

I reached the stage where I got away with everything. I was good value for the newspapers because I blew my own trumpet – too often and far too loud, I now realise – which made good copy for journalists. I was the bloke who brought some welcome fresh air to a game that had been draped with cobwebs, run by men who, if not exactly of the old school tie brigade, had become far too comfortable and smug with their routine. I regarded the game as a business and I was the first one to use the word 'industry' to describe professional football. It was an industry then and it is even more of one today. Now it's huge – possibly too big for its own good, too big to last.

Chairmen remain a major problem. We've gone from the butchers and bakers and candlestick makers to the so-called high-powered businessmen. Some of them seem to have the philosophy that says: 'Just a minute, if I'm going to put substantial money into this club, I want some credit and I want my face on television and in the papers.' Some of them pay themselves fortunes and believe that one of the ways of justifying their existence is to assume a bigger profile and have almost total involvement in the day-to-day operation. I know Leeds United have had their problems over the past couple of years with the court case involving Woodgate and Bowyer, and that the chairman, Peter Ridsdale, has had some public relations work to do.

He made a balls of it, eventually. Having sacked David O'Leary for reasons best known to them and which still bewilder me, Leeds found themselves having to flog some of their top players. They were in the cart, financially – tens, scores of millions in debt. Don't let them blame O'Leary for that – he spent only what Ridsdale and his board allowed him to spend. It was bad management at board level that landed Leeds in deep trouble. The loss of good players didn't help Terry Venables in his efforts to right the ship, but it didn't explain why they slumped towards the relegation end of the table. There was still enough talent at Venables' disposal to produce a side comfortably capable of a place in the top half.

Ah well, at least some justice was done when it all hit the fan. Venables lost his job but no doubt picked up a fortune not only in wages but in compensation as well. Good luck to him! But not only was the manager sacrificed on this occasion, the chairman soon followed as Ridsdale stood down. I say 'justice', because for far too long in my game and on far too many occasions club chairmen have survived situations that were partly created by themselves. If a manager has to be sacked because he's nowhere near good enough, then I believe the man responsible for appointing him should also go – a victim of his own bad judgement. Ridsdale, of course, didn't go because Venables was a bad appointment – in fact I believe he should have stayed as manager until the end of the season. Ridsdale went, presumably, because of the overall circumstances at Elland Road. Up to their necks in debt and with a team under-performing to such an extent that they were actually worried by the possibility of going down. But at least he went. At least a chairman paid for something other than a round of gin-and-tonics.

Sam Longson and the chairmen I worked with in management used to pay for their own petrol but I'd be surprised if today's chairmen do that. They may be somebodies in their business lives, they may be known to people in the commercial and money markets, but if you took away the passes that get them through the front doors of the football grounds, if you removed their status as figureheads of football clubs, they would be nobodies. They could be buskers or vagabonds but football makes them believe they're kings.

Generally speaking, certainly at Hartlepools, Derby and Nottingham, I gave my chairmen fond memories. I made them popular with the public because their football clubs brightened up the lives of everybody in the community and, when you boil it all down, that's what football clubs are for. I did it in various ways. I introduced daft games in training – games from my schoolboy days, passing a ball by hand down two lines of seven players. I won't bore you with the details but cheats were made to run half a lap or do a dozen press-ups. Everybody hated press-ups, especially when he was made to do twelve of 'em with everybody else taking the mickey. Believe it or not, those daft games became as competitive as any match on a Saturday afternoon or a Wednesday night. So was the heading game. Again, Dave Mackay was best of the lot but everybody benefited; they were all slightly better at heading a football by the time we'd finished. Time passed so quickly because the level of enjoyment was so high. There was no routine as such but lots of variety. Only one aspect remained the same – whatever we did, we did it with a ball.

Tactics played very little part in my method of management. I concentrated 90 per cent on how my team played, in preference to wondering about how the opposition would set out their stall. In other words, I worked, taught, coached, cajoled – call it what you want – all with the aim of getting the best out of my lot because, provided I achieved that, I knew that the opposition would have too much on their plate to surprise us. I didn't watch our opponents especially but I had a rough knowledge of them from seeing them on television. I believed in getting the absolute maximum from those in our dressing room. I didn't collect dossiers on opponents like Don Revie did at Leeds. It might sound as though I was lazy, possibly I was, but I had enough on, coping with my team, and wasn't prepared to waste time worrying about anybody else.

For instance, I can't see what difference it makes whether a goalkeeper clears the ball with his left foot or his right. He usually kicks it up into the air, which means one of your guys is going to have to head it. I made sure I had good headers in my teams. Obviously, if we were playing Liverpool, I would know their strengths. I knew their coach, Ronnie Moran, as well as I knew anybody. He had a favourite phrase that he shouted twenty-five times in each half of a match. Over a period of twenty-odd years or more, that's a long time yelling one instruction – 'Keep the ball rolling.'

I knew exactly what he meant – once you stop a ball you invite the opposition to take it off you. A team blossoms only when it has the ball. Flowers need the rain – it's a vital ingredient. Common sense tells you that the main ingredient in football is the ball itself. Common sense told me that, as a manager, you need somebody to get the ball, somebody to keep it, somebody to play it, somebody to put it in the net at one end and somebody to keep it out of the net at the other. Now doesn't that sound simple?

We didn't practise free-kicks in training. We just used the best man for the job depending on where and at what angle free-kicks were awarded during a game. 'Get in on it, a couple of you. Have a look at how the other lot have positioned themselves and if they've lined up badly, use your loaf.' That was about the sum total of my coaching on free-kicks. I signed players who were bright enough to work out those things for themselves. I did like to eliminate some things – particularly shooting at goal from a distance of thirty yards or more. There are very few players who can score from that range. David Beckham has done it a time or two and Stuart Pearce did it for me on several occasions at Forest, whacking in free-kicks with his terrific power. But goals from thirty yards or more are the exception rather than the norm.

I was not in favour of practising our defence of free-kicks, either, but if we conceded a goal from one on the Saturday, first thing Monday morning there would be a familiar to and fro.

'And where were you when that ball went in?' was my first question to the centre-half and back four.

'Well, the centre-forward ran there,' our centre-half would protest, pointing, 'and I went with him.'

'So if he goes for a piss, do you go with him to pull his pants down?'

'What do you mean, Boss?'

So I'd have to explain, spell it out to the lot of them. I know some would call this coaching but I call it management and still do. It was usually the central defender I aimed at.

'You couldn't get to him on the near post because he's quicker than you. So you stand in your patch and if he comes into your patch you deal with it. If he goes ten, fifteen, twenty yards beyond you, it's not your job. It's a full-back's job, somebody from midfield will deal with it.' Football really is a simple game if only people didn't insist on complicating it.

It's the same with crosses from the flanks. Peter Taylor, as a former keeper, used to drum it into me and I used to drum it into the players – the longer a ball takes to come into the box the easier it is to deal with. It's the one that's driven in that does the damage and we had that off to a fine art at Derby and then at Forest with wingers Alan Hinton and John Robertson. Robbo was the complete master. He didn't float crosses very often but if necessary he could float the best crosses known to man. My word, how he could pick out a team-mate! He combined precision with pace.

I prepared my teams almost identically, week in week out, no matter whom we were playing against because, providing we were at our best, I wasn't the slightest bit interested in or concerned about the opposition. My team at its best would be able to deal with them at their best, whomever they might be. I relied on my best wherever possible – the best keeper, the best left-back, the best centre-half, the best centre-forward, the best left winger. You can only have one 'best' in each position, so what was the point in picking anybody else?

I didn't ask any of my players to mark an opponent out of the game, not once. I would give them the instruction, 'You look after your own patch no matter who comes into it.' Obviously, if the other manager told six of his team to play on the right wing, I couldn't leave our left-back to cope with half a dozen, but I'd always tell our right-back, 'You stick to your position whatever the circumstances. I don't care if nobody comes near you, if you don't have a kick all afternoon. You hold your position because one ball will come across at some stage of the ninety minutes and if you're not around it will be the one they put in the net.'

Sometimes one defender would come in at half-time without a bead of sweat while his mate's tongue was hanging out. We weren't influenced by that, we weren't bothered about it. Bear in mind, it works two ways. If the opposition decide to attack one area, it leaves them vulnerable and weak, and open to exploitation. So if you have a good all-round side, a nicely balanced side, you've half a chance. I always had to have a good left-footer somewhere. It meant that however we played and whomever we played, Brian Clough's teams never looked ragged.

All these things slipped nicely into place at Derby. The players learned and I suppose I learned as it all progressed, the promotion to the first division and the walking off with the title three years later. One of my most vivid and satisfying memories of that champion-ship season was my decision to solve the right-back vacancy by chucking in a lad called Steve Powell in the crucial game against Liverpool. He was sixteen years old. We had to fill the gap somehow and Taylor and I took no time at all in deciding the kid should play. 'He's good enough, he's not inclined to freeze or to panic – gerrim in.' That was our attitude and the youngster strolled through the match. We won by the only goal.

If I get angry during these quieter days of my life, it

is usually when I'm reflecting on the championship we won at Derby. We were not given the credit we deserved. The same thing applied at Forest to a certain extent, but there was just some grudging recognition given to our achievement at the Baseball Ground. I'll remind you again – we finished our season before Leeds, who won the FA Cup and would have done the double had they won at Wolves on the Monday after the final. We had our feet up by then. Taylor was in our favourite resort, Cala Millor, with most of the players, and I was in the Scilly Isles with Barbara and the three kids and my mam and dad. If I could take a break during the season, taking time off to be with the family during school half-terms (and I made a habit of it), I could certainly be on holiday while Leeds were trying to fix themselves up with the league title at Molineux. Fix is at least the allegation. There were questions raised about that game, and allegations of attempted bribery, though some of the claims were legally dis- proved later. However, the outcome was a defeat for Revie's side – and the opening of a lot of champagne in the Scilly Isles and in Majorca.

Nearly everybody said that Derby won that championship by default, we hadn't won it as much as Leeds had lost it. Now that still rankles with me, still makes my blood boil because, unless the rules had been changed for that season, they give the championship trophy to the players whose efforts leave them at the top of the table. That's the way it was and that's the way it will always be, and the fact that Leeds didn't finish their fixtures until after ours were complete is a minor and irrelevant detail. Taylor and I worked extremely hard to create the team that ended the season higher than all the rest. It was a genuine and worthy triumph, of as much merit as any that went before it and any that followed it.

I was in the perfect situation to enjoy that incomparable glow of satisfaction – on a beach with my family. Mam was never carried away by what she considered to be the unimportant things in life. She probably got more satisfaction from seeing her washing blowing in the wind before anybody else's in Valley Road on a Monday morning than she got from the championship pennant fluttering above the Baseball Ground. But I think she was pleased that day I became manager of the English League champions. I think I detected an extra little sparkle in her eyes as we sipped the champagne and enjoyed the moment.

Personally, the league title was the ultimate. It was the supreme test of management. Anybody could win a Cup, given a fair wind and a fair slice of luck over a few matches, but finishing top after forty-two games, as it was in those days – that was indisputable evidence. That proved the pedigree of both team and management. They've devalued it in recent years with the top two or three, or even four, qualifying for the Champions League but it is still the competition that singles out the best team in the country. There can be no argument – just as there should have been no argument or protest or grudging acknowledgement when we won it at Derby.

I didn't lose a wink of sleep, mind. I dropped off thinking of the next stage of our development – competing with all the champions from around Europe for the European Cup when it meant far more than it does today. Now as many sides as possible are involved in order to generate as much money as possible, fat cats getting fatter and fourth-placed sides being involved in something wrongly called a Champions League. I don't suppose you could call it a Champions, Runners-up and Third and Fourth-place League but that's what it amounts to. It's a joke and not very funny but it makes money so they're all happy with it.

It was a genuine competition in the seventies. There was no league format to start with. You were in the hat among the very best and you survived or were knocked out with no second chance in the next stage. You sank or you swam, and our lot at Derby just couldn't wait to get in the water. I certainly couldn't – I immediately became obsessed with the European Cup, as obsessed with it as Sir Alex Ferguson could ever be. I wanted to rub shoulders with the likes of Juventus, Real Madrid and Benfica. I'd come a long way from Valley Road but I knew I wouldn't feel out of place in the slightest.

CHAPTER 6

THE BIGGEST MISTAKE OF MY LIFE

They say that time heals but it doesn't, not entirely – it just helps you put things into some kind of perspective. I've had nearly thirty years to think about the events of 1973 and time has not eased much of the pain. If I live to be a hundred, I don't suppose it ever will.

Derby County were equipped, capable and ready to take Europe by storm. All time has done has been to convince me that we would have won the European Cup at the first time of asking but for the distasteful events that occurred in Turin during the first leg of our semi-final against Juventus. It wasn't that we lost 3–1 although, obviously, that was bad enough. I believed then and still believe that, one way or another, the match was bent. My immediate reaction on the night has been well documented, with my quote about 'cheating, fucking Italian bastards' – no, I'm not much calmer when I recall that night, even now.

Nothing has been proved despite the official investigation that took place later. It wasn't established whether or not the German referee had actually been bribed. It was never established, as far as I know, why one of our opponents had apparently been into the referee's room prior to the match and during the interval. Something else I'll never know is why Roy McFarland and Archie Gemmill were booked before we got to half-time. The offences were seen by the referee but they were by no means obvious to anybody from Derby. What we did know was that both had been cautioned earlier in the tournament and would therefore have to sit out the second leg against the Italian champions. As far as I was concerned, the entire episode stank the place out. We had been done but not fairly and squarely by a team worthy of a 3–1 margin – I could have lived with that. Defeat is never easy to take but I have always been able to accept it providing it's been inflicted legitimately. To name just one rotten aspect of the game, it is corrupt in my book for players to dive like dolphins at the slightest pretext. I close my eyes and think of that bloody awful night in Turin and what I see is the majority of the opposition flinging themselves all over the place and conning the referee time after time after time. It might have become a little exaggerated in my mind but the overall picture hasn't. The effect has lasted as long as the pictures from the match itself.

Peter Taylor was just as incensed as I was and as a result he had his collar felt by the local police.

Fortunately, his arrest didn't last very long. If he'd managed to get hold of that referee, the consequences might have detained him in Italy for the rest of his days.

A night like that one in Turin could sour you. It could destroy your belief in your own industry. Thankfully, my belief in the integrity of the English game – despite what happened with those two defenders at Middlesbrough – and my belief in myself and my team was too strong for one evening of skulduggery to harm it for long. But the heartbreak was to become even more intense, unbearable, by the time the second leg came around.

It just happened to be on the night of my birthday. Hope didn't spring eternal exactly, but we still had hope enough of turning things round and making it through to the final. No team liked coming to the Baseball Ground. Tight, intimate and intimidating, with the crowd so close to the pitch, the unique atmosphere we created was worth a goal at least to Derby. It could be hell on earth to the opposition and I don't care how experienced they were. But time can't alter the facts – our centre-forward Roger Davies was sent off and Alan Hinton missed a penalty. Of course we were dejected at being knocked out of the competition but it was fury at what happened in Turin rather than frustration at what happened in the second leg that dominated our mood.

Just when you think things can't get worse, they invariably do. We'd been knocked out of the European Cup on my birthday but a phone call reduced all that, even the things that occurred in Italy, to meaningless trivia. The late-night call was from our Joe breaking the terrible news that Mam had died. We had all realised that she was dying from cancer but it was still a devastating blow. You don't need reminding yet again about my feelings for my mam and the influence she had on my life. Knowing all that, you still can't begin to imagine how I felt when I picked up that phone and heard our Joe's voice. I was empty – thankful, oh so thankful, that Barbara and my family were around me but I still had a feeling, strangely, of being alone. Your mam is someone who's always been there and should always be there. She's a guide, a reassurance, your best friend and the finest teacher you'll ever come across. I know mine was. I also know I haven't always lived my life in the way she showed me I should. She was seventy-three at the end. Dad was eighty-one when we lost him four years later. Time doesn't end the sense of loneliness; it just helps to make you a little less lonely.

It was a sad, tragic end to that European adventure of ours; sadder, in personal terms, than I could ever have expected, but sad, too, from a professional point of view. Derby had been capable of going all the way, as we proved in the early stages of the tournament. We were getting through without a problem, we were cruising past the opposition, we were doing it with our eyes closed – or I was, literally.

We liked a soft pitch at our place. It wasn't soft enough for my liking the night before Eusebio came to town with his Portuguese mates from Benfica. I knew

what was needed to get the likeliest winning performance from that team of ours at home. Those were the
days when Brian Clough took more water with it! I used
to water our pitch more times than the groundsman
did. Half the time nobody knew I was doing it because I
went back at night. I had the keys to just about everything and everywhere at the Baseball Ground. If I
needed to see in the interests of accuracy, I knew how to
switch on the floodlights, but the night prior to the
Benfica game I did it in the dark. We didn't have
sprinklers; we had two big hosepipes that were equivalent in power to the ones firemen use. I would switch
them on, sit back on the terrace steps and let them do
their job. Usually, I'd leave them for no longer than
twenty minutes because the pitch couldn't take any
more water than that so quickly. Unfortunately, or
fortunately as things turned out, on that night I
dropped off. Hey, I was a busy man working a lot of
hours in a week, and I had three small children at home.
Life can get tiring even for somebody who believed he
was a genius.

I don't know how long I slept while the hoses gushed
their gallons. All I know is that I woke up drenched and
with enough water on that ground to have staged an
Olympic diving event from the top board!

You probably know the story but this one's worth
re-telling because it involved the establishment – Sir
Stanley Rous, President of FIFA, no less. Apart from
ticking me off for my shouting during the match, he
had taken one look at the pitch and wondered how it

could have been inches deep in mud when there had been no rain whatsoever at his hotel just up the road. I explained that the weather could be like that in Derby. We often had torrential downpours at the Baseball Ground when they didn't get a drop half a mile away in town. It was one of the wonders of mother nature.

It did the trick, I know that. Benfica couldn't live with us or the pitch, the crowd, the atmosphere and particularly the football we played. In the second leg, despite their refusal to let us have the ball in the early stages, we didn't need a hosepipe to douse their optimism. We just got a grip, defended the way you're supposed to defend in Europe and clung to a goalless draw. We'd beaten one of the big names of continental football, one of the magical names. We'd held our own in the Stadium of Light, one of the legendary venues of Europe. We'd survived and prospered partly because of what I'd done in the dark. Don't ever try telling me there is nothing to be gained by falling asleep on the job.

Chairmen change. Sam Longson changed very quickly from the friendly, generous old man who regarded me as the son he'd never had, who bought us gifts and often lent Barbara and me his gleaming Mercedes, to a vulnerable individual who put his own interests, image and reputation before those of the club. He'd often tell me to calm down when my name hit the papers under some controversial, provocative headline, which it did on a regular basis. He'd occasionally suggest I gave it more thought before I opened my mouth. But I was popular with the media. I was doing the TV panels with the likes of Jimmy Hill, Jack Charlton, Malcolm Allison and Bill Shankly. It was like a football *Who's Who* on the box at that time, and I was usually the one who said something that was seized on by the press. I never did see the point of going on television, expected to voice an honest opinion, and then saying next to nothing or being cautious and particularly careful just to avoid upsetting somebody. There are too many supposed pundits who do exactly that now. What a life! Get yourself on TV, get paid a small fortune, smile a lot and say next to nowt. Now that is nice work if you can get it.

I don't know whether it was jealousy, a wee bit of envy, but Sam Longson's attitude cooled towards Taylor and me. I was forever in the papers or on TV, spouting about every footballing subject under the sun, and some people might have gained the impression that I was in charge of everything at Derby. I was told that Longson started to go around insisting in that gravel voice of his, 'I'm the one who runs Derby County – not Brian Clough.' That was what started the rot, that and the arrival of a director called Jack Kirkland.

Pete Taylor had already told me to beware of the club secretary, the dapper little Stuart Webb. Taylor was brilliant at detecting those we should be wary of – directors or any club employee. We needed to be able to trust everybody – from the chairman to the secretary to the bloke who drove the team bus and the ladies who made the tea or did the laundry.

Taylor was suspicious of Kirkland from the outset, an inquisitive so-and-so poking his nose into this and that. So we had the secretary trying to do a balancing act as a friend of the management and the boardroom, we had the chairman realising that I had too big a profile for his liking and we had a nosey old bugger as a new director, who seemed determined to find out exactly how this successful club was being run.

We feared nobody as a team – we were that good. Not even the prospect of playing Manchester United at Old Trafford worried us in the slightest. We had respect for them because we had respect for all opponents but we had so much faith in the collective ability at Derby – mine, Taylor's, coach Jimmy Gordon's and particularly the team's – that we honestly believed we could beat anybody anywhere, unless there was a German referee, that is! Yet Kirkland wanted to stick his nose into it all.

One October afternoon when we'd gone to Old Trafford and beaten United, Taylor and I accepted their chairman Louis Edwards' invitation to the boardroom, which wasn't our usual style. Get the match over, get on the coach as quickly as possible and get home – that was our familiar routine. Who knows, if we had followed our usual pattern that day, we might not have made what I consider to have been the worst decision of our lives.

It was the beginning of the end when Taylor revealed on the journey back to Derby that Kirkland had called him over and said he had to meet him on the Monday to explain the details and the precise nature of his duties. We had won a league championship, we had carried that club from nowhere to the top of the tree, we had been cheated out of the European Cup at the semi-final stage, and this interfering bugger wanted to know what Taylor did for his living. I could have told him what he did – he had helped build a football club that had enough appeal and popularity for Jack Kirkland to want to join its board of directors.

Taylor kept the meeting and was convinced that the directors, or a section of them, were attempting to unsettle me by getting at him. He had been humiliated by a man who was not entitled to question anything unless he'd been asking Peter for the time of day. They talk about the end of a beautiful friendship – well this was the end of a fantastic relationship between a club and the management team who had transformed it. It was a relationship that I cherished.

I had been interviewed for the job of Barcelona manager along the way. You don't turn down the chance of at least talking to a club of that magnitude if you've any sense. But I think I blew my chances when I was asked how I would respond to a situation in which more than 100,000 fans were waving white hand-kerchiefs in my direction.

'I'd have learned enough Spanish to be able to tell them all to piss off,' I said, or something as equally silly as that. The same bloke was reassured by Taylor – 'Don't worry, he'll be able to look after anything the crowd can send his way. In any case, he'll have 100,000 of them waving flags and dancing the flamenco by the time he's finished. They'll be celebrating and you'll be holding trophies and we'll have taken all the worries off your shoulders.' It was a very persuasive attitude and it often made people feel a million dollars, but it didn't work on that occasion.

Neither did my attempts to steer Peter away from his conclusion that we were not fully appreciated at Derby, that the board were after our blood, that what Kirkland had done had sent out the clear message that we should quit and be on our way. He wouldn't budge and it was me who did the quitting with no fuss, no looking over my shoulder. It was straight into the boardroom and straight out with it – 'I want you to accept our resignations.' I seem to remember one voice, maybe two, quietly asking me to reconsider but Longson's wasn't among them. I didn't wait for a yes or a no. I went to tell Taylor that we had quit. There was no money, no compensation, we were out but we knew we'd have no problem getting another job.

What we didn't know was that there would be so many people involved in that extraordinary campaign to get us reinstated. No football club had witnessed scenes like those ever before and, to my knowledge, nothing like them has been seen since. There were public marches through the town with protest banners everywhere and protest meetings. The ground was besieged by supporters and the media for days on end. The players, my players, led the protests and even threatened a sit-down strike. It was brilliantly organised and well executed, which is not that surprising because I was behind most of it. Having resigned, you might wonder why I took so much trouble involving myself with the revolution that swept the town. Feelings really were running that high, believe me. It was revolution and in my heart I thought those directors would invite us back. Never underestimate the toughness of a man who earns his living from stone quarries. Sam Longson didn't flinch and neither did his fellow directors apart from the late Mike Keeling who had become a good friend and who quit the board when Taylor and I stormed out.

The scenes at Derby were astounding – club officials locked themselves in the boardroom and, too scared to come out, had to relieve themselves in a champagne bucket. My appearance at the home game the following Saturday set off a crowd reaction as loud as the one that had accompanied the defeat of Benfica, and I went on the Michael Parkinson show that very night. Then the appointment of Dave Mackay as my successor was announced despite captain Roy McFarland's phone call warning him not to take the job because they were trying to get Taylor and me reinstated. The warning failed, Mackay came striding in as only a man of his courage and reputation could and, as I mentioned, was eventually to win Derby another championship.

That achievement was further proof of the mistake Taylor and I made. It was the biggest professional mistake of my career. We should have stayed, ridden the storm and seen it out on the strength of the talent that had turned Derby County into the football club with the greatest potential in the country. I'm prepared to go as far as to say that if we'd stayed at Derby, they would have been the Manchester United of the present day, certainly in terms of success on the field. What a thing to be saying considering they recently lost their status in the top division of the English game.

When we left, Derby had the youngest side up there and it was a team of outstanding quality. We had Roy McFarland who was undoubtedly the best centre-half in the country, and Colin Todd can't have been too bad seeing that he gained twenty-seven England caps in his time. We had John McGovern, everybody's idea of the perfect midfield player. He played for Scotland and was to become the Nottingham Forest captain who was presented with the European Cup two years in succession. We had John O'Hare, another Scottish international, at centre-forward with Kevin Hector alongside him, and he was good enough to play for England. We had Alan Hinton on the left-wing and I'm telling you that if England could call on anybody nearly as effective as him in that position today, we wouldn't have been talking about a weakness on the left flank before the team left to play in the 2002 World Cup. So we had enough – more than enough. Other teams would have progressed but we'd have kept pace and gone ahead of them. Having some of the best players already, we'd have kept winning and the better players from other clubs would have wanted to join us. Success really does breed success.

Had Taylor and I been in our right minds and stayed at

Derby, no team would have been allowed to run away with things, to dominate the game in the way Manchester United have done in recent years. Inevitably, the bigger clubs would have joined the picture – Arsenal, Liverpool and of course Manchester United among them – but little Derby would have established themselves among the élite and grown until they were as big as any of them.

I wish I had tried to prolong my playing career after the injury at Sunderland. I know I should have prolonged my managerial career at the Baseball Ground. Resigning when we did was crazy – I can see that even more clearly now than I did ten years ago. Anger impaired my vision. For a moment or two I lost sight of what I had created and threw it all away. If I'd stayed at Derby, I wouldn't have won one thing for two years or five years – I'd have won everything for ten years at least. Nobody could have touched us. Don't forget when it came to signing players, we were the best in the business; and I was undoubtedly the best at getting maximum performance from those at our disposal. As for running the club, we ran it from A to Z. We had the formula for lasting success. One man discovered penicillin and we had discovered the equivalent in the footballing world.

No, time hasn't healed the wound I inflicted on myself by quitting the job for what amounted to selfish reasons of pride and ego – my conceit again although it was Taylor's idea originally. Boiling it all down, we left for childish reasons.

In those days we believed everything we did was

right. We made decisions instantly. Taylor wasn't a wilting flower as an assistant manager. Don't forget he had been a pal of mine for years. He was a strong personality and could be persuasive. When he said he was packing in, I took it for granted that he *was* packing in. If I'd been slightly more mature, a few years older, I wouldn't have gone along with him. I'd have called round to see him on that Saturday night or the Sunday morning and said, 'Hey, come on. Look at what we've built together, look at what we've got, look at how far we could go with this club. Let's sit down and give it some serious thought.' Peter influenced me almost 100 per cent. We had nothing else in the pipeline but quitting is made easier when you know alternative offers will not be in terribly short supply. We made a huge mistake by sticking to our guns.

If Taylor was obsessed with anything beyond building football teams and winning matches, it was money. It wasn't long before he came to me and announced, 'I've got us a deal. I've got us fifteen grand between us. We can take over at Brighton.'

I should have seen it coming. He always wanted to finish his working life and end up retired at the seaside.

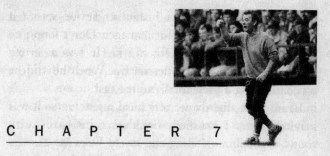

CLOUGHIE

CHAPTER 7

IN NEED OF A FRIEND

Whenever people recall that I managed Brighton for thirty-two matches – and won only twelve, incidentally – they still believe it was just a convenience, a temporary easy-picking to tide me over until a bigger job came along. They were wrong to think it at the time and they are still wrong to believe it today. I was sincere in my agreement to join Mike Bamber, the pleasantest and finest chairman who ever employed me.

It is thirty years since I made that huge mistake at Derby and dropped two divisions to pick up my career in the third, travelling from Derby to the south coast. Despite the luxury of life in a posh hotel, it was still a chore to be away from Barbara and the children for several days on end. The kids' schooling meant that Barbara had to spend the majority of the time in the East Midlands. To begin with, Taylor was not around a lot, either. But I knew all this when we accepted Bamber's offer. I was not a man to go for a stop–gap post, never was and never could be. If I went in for something, it was with both eyes open and fully intent on committing myself totally to the task.

Bamber was the owner of a local nightclub so it was inevitable that I brushed shoulders occasionally with showbiz people, including the lovely Dora Bryan who told us we could stay at her house in Brighton, Bruce Forsyth and the late Les Dawson. He left a telling impression on me when we were introduced by limiting our conversation to, 'Sorry, but I'm bloody well working.' And so he was. He was perfectly entitled to avoid pointless niceties at a time like that. Maybe I learned it from him; throughout the rest of my career in management, I had no time for polite chat when I was working.

It was by no means the only lesson I learned at Brighton. A 4–0 defeat by Walton and Hersham in the first round of the FA Cup was the first time any such thing had happened to me. My system had to get used to shocks. The scoreline of a home game against Bristol Rovers is etched in my mind as deeply as the two European Cup finals I was to win years later. We lost 8–2, and I'll tell you why we lost 8–2. It was not just because we had a terrible team with players who couldn't play. It was because they were petrified of me.

There is still a wrong impression about Brian Clough in English football. Too many idiots, some of them respected observers of the game, still argue that fear was my biggest weapon as a manager, a weapon and a means of motivation. That's another chip on my shoulder that has grown bigger in retirement. Of all the things said about me, of all the attempts to explain my success, that one is the biggest load of crap I have ever heard in my life. My teams, my Derby and Nottingham Forest teams, could not have played the kind of football they produced if they'd been frightened. There was not an ounce of fear in their game – they played with a kind of freedom and sheer joy that you rarely see from teams today.

I tried to avoid instilling fear rather than imposing it but that day at Brighton when we conceded eight goals, I knew they were frightened because they were all inferior players who had never known success and never encountered anybody like me. If I'd told them to cut their wrists I believe every single one of them would have done it right there in the dressing room and that was before the match! They were rigid, virtually frozen to the spot by fear and out on the pitch there was so much apprehension that they couldn't lift their legs, let alone raise a gallop.

Offers of alternative employment came along. I could have been an MP after receiving a second invitation from the Labour party to contest Manchester's Moss Side against young Winston Churchill; and I was offered the national team manager's job in Iran. This was in the days of the Shah. There was much for me to admire in that country, not least his Thoroughbred horses, but the life was not for me; nor for that matter was my life in Brighton. I was too often away from

Barbara and the bairns, and for the first time, I sensed that Peter Taylor was not quite as full of himself as usual, or particularly happy in his work.

As luck would have it, the big offer came along. Don Revie was leaving Leeds to be manager of England and they wanted me to take over. I jumped at it but Taylor didn't. I've thought a lot about his reasons for saying 'we'll be fine' at Brighton, urging me to give it another season and insisting he would 'stay put' when I demanded a clear answer. I've thought about it long and hard in retirement. I discovered Mike Bamber had offered him more money to stay and I always knew Pete fancied a crack at management in his own right. He never did learn about that, did he? He had another crack at solo management at Derby after retiring from Forest, and it was never going to work out for him there, either. So, just as it was his initial instinct for us to walk away from all we had created at Derby, it was Pete who broke up our partnership. I went; he stayed down south.

Money would have got Pete to Leeds. It might have cost their chairman Manny Cussins a few grand but money could have lured him to Elland Road. I think one reason he wanted to stay on the south coast was because I had just helped get his daughter a job on the local paper. She was happy, Pete had everybody together in his apartment in Brighton and, as I was well aware, he'd always wanted to be beside the seaside. Even in our early days together, whenever conversation drifted towards eventual retirement Pete would say,

'I'm going to keep heading south every year. In the end after landing a job on the coast, that's where I'll retire. That's my ambition. And if Scarborough was in the south, I'd pack in and go and live there right now.' Maybe it was because Pete hailed from Nottingham. Can you get further away from the seaside than that? Strange that he would later abandon his intended 'retirement home' in Brighton and return to his roots, joining up with me again and going on to achieve our greatest moments together with Forest.

At least I had a chance of getting a look at the European Cup with Leeds. Pete had no chance of cracking management on his own, however appealing life in Brighton might have been. He had no chance whatsoever.

As it turned out, I had no chance either, not the way I went about taking over from Don Revie. I don't know whether my sacking after forty-four days was a record but it was no real surprise in view of the way I tackled the job, trying to do in minutes what should have taken months, maybe even years. I went at it like a bull at a fence. I rushed it. Now I realise that I blew it. I've said before that they disliked me at Elland Road, the majority of the players that is, but I reckon they actually hated my guts. Reflection tells me that the biggest mistake of all was my eagerness to accept the job in the first place. Leeds weren't for me and I wasn't for them.

You don't need reminding of too much of the detail or the way I had criticised that Leeds side, one of the most cynical and dirtiest as well as talented I had ever seen. I was a big admirer of Revie's but I had serious reservations about the way the 'family', as he called it, sometimes went about their business. Leeds, with Billy Bremner, Johnny Giles, Norman Hunter, big Jack Charlton and Allan Clarke up front, had players in every position to make other managers envious. They were a wonderful side who set a wonderful example for the most part. In fact, I had the impression that Leeds could have been more dazzling still had Revie been less systematic and allowed them off that tight rein of his.

They paid a price for their cynicism, their intimidation of referees and the over-physical element of their game. It undermined public respect for what they achieved. They became notorious and are still remembered for being 'dirty Leeds' rather than for the terrific football they played. That's a shame, but it is also a kind of justice.

My criticism of them meant I was confronted by a seething, resentful, spiteful dressing room when I arrived on my first morning, fresh from holiday in Cala Millor, with my boys Simon and Nigel for company. It makes me flinch just a little to this day, remembering that scene. It was like walking straight into an ambush. You could have cut the atmosphere with a knife. Revie might have left but his presence and influence was everywhere. I was daft enough to believe that a bit of tongue-in-cheek banter might ease the situation – a word about Hunter and Giles clattering people, a wise-crack to point out that if a racehorse had had as many injuries as Scottish winger Eddie Gray he'd have been put down months ago. Nobody was laughing. It's a well-known saying of mine that football management can be a lonely job. It was never lonelier than at Elland Road where I was made to feel like the arch enemy. I felt something worse than misery – I was desolate.

The extent of my misery possibly impaired my better judgement because I ignored the sound advice of scout Tony Collins who urged me to take my time with the changes I had in mind. He warned me not to be too hasty, that Leeds didn't take kindly to anybody who appeared to be rocking their boat. I just ploughed on through the waves and was determined that one or two were going overboard. Despite his international caps for Scotland, I believed we needed a better goalkeeper than David Harvey. I wanted Giles out of the place too. I certainly knew he had been Revie's recommendation for the manager's job and he was extremely influential. The other players had enormous respect for the little Irishman and with good reason. My plan to flog him to Tottenham backfired when Giles turned down the chance to go to White Hart Lane, spurning an opportunity to be schooled as the likely successor to Bill Nicholson.

Never has a man given me less time to get him to know and to like me, or dislike me for that matter. I'm sure it wasn't anything personal; it was just that he thought he was going to get the Leeds job and knew that the rest of the players were in favour of him getting it. Instead, the club brought me in – not just an outsider, gate-crashing the happy family, but an enemy, a man who was against almost everything that Leeds stood for. If Bremner had disliked me – and I don't think he did – he would have let me know straight out. Having begun to wonder why Leeds had appointed me at all, I asked Manny Cussins. He said, 'When a group of players is prepared to go on strike for a manager, that manager has got to be good' – a reference to Derby of course. He could also have said that any manager who walked out on a team as good as that one at Derby couldn't have been much of a judge.

I never did get to know John Giles, still don't. In view of all the circumstances, I talked less at Leeds than in any job I ever had. I think I must have been waiting for their fabled professionalism to show itself. What I did know about Giles was the extent of his talent in midfield. He could grab hold of a match, tuck it in his back pocket and carry it around with him. He didn't need to find space; it was as if space found him. It was always available to him – a tribute to his perception, footballing brain and the wonderful natural instinct that separates great players from the rest. He could play a pass of the most delicate nature and perfect precision. He had the reputation of being one who could deliver immediate justice on the pitch.

Most little players were aggressive players, probably making up for their limited physique. Bremner had his nasty side, too. Bobby Collins, Giles's predecessor as the fulcrum of the team, was another and I had two similar types in Willie Carlin and Archie Gemmill. For all that aspect of his game, I respected Giles because of his tremendous ability. His knowledge of the game was proved in his short time in management at West Brom and I wish now that things could have been different at Leeds and we could have got our heads and our talents together over a longish period of time. Who knows, Giles could have become my Peter Taylor. He'd certainly have needed to get that close if he was going to have any input into the management of Leeds United while I was there. Who knows what might have happened if we'd got together.

I know one thing – had Taylor not opted to remain at Brighton he would have twigged the situation, possibly within minutes. He could sniff them out because he was what I called a sitter-back. He'd take a look at the situation from a quiet corner or in a crowded dressing room. He'd look for telltale signs that indicated whether someone was with us or against us. It didn't take him long and he was rarely wrong.

I wasn't exactly a mug in the game. After all, I'd won the championship at Derby in such a short time and was still under forty years of age. I hadn't broken any eggs at Brighton but that didn't really matter because, football-wise, nobody knew where Brighton was. But I felt hostility from just about every quarter at Leeds apart from Allan Clarke, 'Sniffer' as they affectionately called the England international striker.

I suppose there were others who didn't necessarily dislike me – Bremner, for a start. What a player! What a tragedy that he was to die so suddenly and so young. Bill Shankly always rated Billy among the greats and I go along with that. But Clarkey was the one who offered me some warmth and comfort. He was the one who showed genuine friendship, and friendship was in extremely short supply.

Those people who believe I instilled fear at the clubs I worked for should have seen me during those forty-four days. I couldn't have imposed fear at Leeds if I'd tried. They had endured and overcome all the fear, apprehension and uncertainty that go through the minds of successful players during the winning of championships, cups and European tournaments. Leeds had done it all; they were the kings of English football. They weren't threatened, any of them, because they felt they were bigger than me. When I went to Derby and Brighton, everybody looked up to me. When I went to Leeds, the boot was on the other foot. I was the one looking up because they were the stars – internationals wherever you cared to look, on the team-sheet and off it.

For all that, I knew I was inheriting a side on its last legs. They were getting old together. Revie had left several contracts still to be negotiated and players around the thirty mark worry about their futures. But nobody at Leeds was more worried than I was. I didn't feel the remotest connection with the team. Just before the Charity Shield match at Wembley, the game between the champions and FA Cup winners that traditionally kicks off the season, I telephoned Revie and told him to lead them out because Leeds was his team not mine, even though I knew I would be passing up the chance to march out alongside Bill Shankly and his beloved Liverpool. Revie, of course, declined my invitation. Invitation? I suppose I was thinking more of myself than of him at the time. It was all part of that feeling of detachment from the club who had hired me as the best man for their job.

If I felt sorry for myself that day, I was to feel even sorrier for Kevin Keegan. You'll remember the famous picture of him, flinging down his shirt as he was sent off. Now for Keegan to throw down the cherished shirt of Liverpool the circumstances had to be extreme and they were. For once, I fully understood the reaction of a player who had taken too much intimidation and physical bruising. Bremner, my captain, had whacked him uphill and down dale. Keegan snapped. He could take no more. He retaliated and got himself sent off alongside Bremner. Oh, what a lovely day that turned out to be!

You never need friends more than when you're lonely. Take my time? I couldn't get friendly faces into Elland Road quickly enough. I signed John McGovern and John O'Hare from Derby and Duncan McKenzie, that flamboyant striker – eccentric may be a better description – from Forest.

McGovern's talents were not as obvious as those of the other two – his immense physical and moral courage, his willingness to put in his lot whatever the circumstances, his total trustworthiness and reliability, his ability to play a pass. They humiliated him at Leeds, players and crowd alike. John was to have the last laugh in years to come as the player who twice accepted the

European Cup as the winning captain. But at the time of his Leeds experience, it was difficult to imagine that anything could compensate for what that lot put him through, and it had been my fault because I was the one who put him in what became an intolerable situation.

I was still determined to steer the boat through the stormy waters even if it meant rocking the bloody thing from side to side in the process. I was convinced we needed a better goalkeeper and that's what sank my boat altogether. Typical me, I informed Harvey that I wanted to sign Peter Shilton. The balloon went up, the boat went down – forty-four days, over and out.

Thank heavens for Colin Lawrence. It was my dear friend Colin who helped me come to terms with the fact that I had been sacked. In denting my ego and showing me the door, Leeds United did me the biggest favour of my professional life.

I had signed a four-year contract and told Manny Cussins, 'You'll have to square it up.'

'Right,' Cussins replied, but I bet he didn't realise what he'd let himself in for; 'grossing-up' I think it was called, or something like that. Whatever the term, what I do know is that Leeds signed an agreement that committed them to paying all my tax for the following three years. Instead of costing them £25,000 as a pay-off, it finally worked out at £98,000. I came out of Elland Road a little crestfallen professionally, but quite rich. I was financially secure for the first time in my life and I knew that whatever job came my way, I would be able to do it with complete peace of mind.

CHAPTER 8

I SHOULD HAVE
TRIED TO UNDERSTAND

The feeling of independence and security that Leeds
gave me together with the sack was a big factor in
winning so much during my eighteen years as manager
of Nottingham Forest, not least the league championship and two European Cups. It meant I could
approach the job without a financial care in the world. I
could follow my instincts and hunches and gut feelings
and to hell with the consequences should it all go
wrong.

Not much did go wrong, of course. It was success
virtually all the way once I'd settled in, sorted things
out and freshened up a decaying club that was dying on
its feet when I breezed into the place in January 1975.
They were struggling too close to the wrong end of the
second division, with not enough players in the dressing room who could kick a ball properly or head a ball

105

adequately, let alone with the ability to play the game. Isn't it odd to look back to that time with the reminder that when I arrived at the City Ground, Martin O'Neill and John Robertson were among the players who were up for sale. Look at them now, doing great things together in charge of Celtic. How times do change.

The Leeds experience, for all the benefit it did my bank account and peace of mind, also savaged my ego. The sack does hurt, no matter how substantial the compensation money, which goes some way towards cushioning the fall. So it was some time before I was able to walk on water even though my very first game in charge was an FA Cup replay at Tottenham that we won against the odds. We followed it up with another victory at Fulham on the Saturday, but if the people of Nottingham, the Forest supporters, believed the miracle was happening immediately, they were in for a rude awakening. By the end of that initial season, we'd won just three out of seventeen matches, including that Cup-tie at White Hart Lane. We were bloody fortunate not to get relegated to the third division.

A sorting-out process was necessary, with bodies in as well as out. You don't change a stagnant pool by staring at the water; you have to disturb it – eliminate the pollution and introduce the elements that can make it fresh again. Well, I turfed out the crap and added some players who could actually play football to operate alongside the likes of Tony Woodcock, Ian Bowyer, O'Neill and Robertson, and the right-back, Viv Anderson.

Little things, the odd moment or two from the past, give you a glow of satisfaction on rainy days in retirement when there is little else to do but sit and ponder. Going back to Leeds to re-sign John O'Hare and John McGovern is a memory that still manages to keep me warm when the central heating's gone off. Leeds' directors didn't know what they had in their possession with those two. That's why I was able to buy them back for less than I'd forked out on Leeds' behalf in the first place. They were familiar faces, and had undoubted ability. A manager cannot surround himself with too many people of genuine calibre, which was why Jimmy Gordon, sacked by Leeds when they kicked me out, was recruited to the ranks at the City Ground. Trainer? Coach? The job title didn't matter to me. Coach, if you like. Whatever the handle, Jimmy was brought in because he was as honest as the day is long, knew the game inside out and was good with players. I'd seen all that in him during my younger days at Middlesbrough where Jimmy was among the leading professionals.

I suppose eighth place wasn't too bad for my first complete season in the job but there was still an important element missing. Peter Taylor had staked everything on promotion at Brighton and had just failed. Almost as much for his ability to make me laugh as for his ability as a talent spotter, for whatever reason, for all reasons, Taylor's contribution to the revolution that took place at Nottingham Forest cannot be overestimated. The flight to Majorca to see him at his villa was possibly the most productive flight I ever made. His coyness was just a front. Despite that ambition of his to retire by the seaside, I knew he would leap at the chance to help manage Nottingham Forest, his home-town club, no matter how far it happened to be from the nearest beach. Once again, I wasn't wrong.

Players didn't fall off trees to land at Nottingham Forest. We had to search for them, high and low. You name it, Taylor and I did it. There were long car journeys, sometimes to non-league matches, defying the elements on a piss-it-down Tuesday night somewhere. Often we also defied the majority opinion of others watching the man we had targeted.

If there was a magic formula to our style of management, we were the ones who invented it. We dragged the new recruits from all corners, nooks and crannies and the occasional dog track in our time. Frank Clark, a left-back, that rarest of breeds, came on a free transfer from Newcastle at the age of thirty-two – the bargain of all bargains. Larry Lloyd came from Coventry where he seemed to have disappeared after managing to earn himself an England cap or two at Liverpool. Kenny Burns came from Birmingham after Taylor had him shadowed to his favourite greyhound stadium and reported that the Scot with a harsh reputation for violence, drink and gambling was not that type of lad at all. I still talk to him from time to time to this day. Garry Birtles was signed from Long Eaton for about two grand, and Archie Gemmill was nicked from Derby for twenty-five grand. Oh yes, and there was the small matter of £270,000 for Peter Shilton from Stoke.

We were 'mad' in many people's eyes to spend a record fee on him but Taylor and I knew our history in advance. History now tells us that Shilton was worth twice the price. We weren't mad at all; we were magic.

You will notice from that handful of names, and there are too many others to mention, that there was a familiar, tried-and-trusted formula – a goalkeeper, two centre-halves in this instance, and a centre-forward. There they are. There's part of the secret, that's the framework, the backbone, those are the key components in the skeleton of any side.

Our conceit and fanaticism were vital as well. We needed the belief that we could do no wrong. Taylor may have been different from me but he was still a conceited man. It didn't come across publicly because he rarely opened his mouth but if ever he'd been offered a part in a film he'd have been the one with the gun. I'd have been the unfortunate so-and-so who was seen loading it and then handing it to the police, saying, 'This is the weapon I used to shoot the fella.'

That was the difference between us and it was a combination that worked brilliantly. I was totally blind to pitfalls and criticism; Peter was the shrewdy, slightly in the background if not the shadows. I've lost count of the number of occasions when he put up an idea and I followed it through in my inimitable, sod-the-lot-of-'em kind of way.

'Do you know what you're doing?' Pete would say.

'Of course I know what I'm bloody well doing.'

'Well, you'll never get away with that.'

One example, back in our Derby days, was the signing of David Nish, Leicester's left-back, another of those rarities, whom we turned into an international player. I actually gate-crashed a board meeting at Leicester – breezed straight in, large as life, and told them I'd come to sign Nish. Well, I had. I wasn't in Leicester for a night out so I didn't see the point of beating about the bush. Whether those directors were so gobsmacked, so taken aback at the sudden arrival of this loud-mouthed impostor, I didn't know and I didn't give a toss. All that mattered was that we signed David Nish, just as we signed so many from right under other people's noses. I got away with it.

To be honest, I did ride the wind as a manager and at times too close to it. It didn't worry me because I didn't think I was doing anything wrong. I would never claim to be an angel but if I did offend people in the process of my work, I just wallowed in my conceit, believing nobody had been harmed. I certainly didn't harm anyone intentionally.

My manner and our success meant I made enemies and Taylor would say, 'You do know they don't like you, don't you?' He was talking about various people, other managers, directors, the authorities. 'They don't like you because they're jealous of you.' I didn't recognise that but Peter did. If I made enemies, it was because of our success, not because I'd done them out of ten quid or fiddled them at cards.

The point I'm coming to is that the Clough–Taylor managerial partnership was unique. It remains unique to this day, partly because we could not be copied and partly because if anybody had attempted it, they would have fallen flat on their faces. However, there is a partnership in British football management that bears a striking resemblance. Martin O'Neill and John Robertson might not be carbon copies of Clough and Taylor but they look like turning out to be pretty similar and the next best thing. What an impact they have had since arriving at Parkhead, including back-to-back league champion-ships. Celtic have not been able to dominate Scottish football in such a way for twenty years, even if they did lose out to Rangers in 2002–03.

As I said, they were already at Forest when I bowled into the place, on the transfer list, fed up with the feeling of decline around the City Ground. They stayed because they had talent, and that talent was to help them win medals they can never have imagined they'd win in their weirdest dreams.

I've said often enough that I wasn't sure why I perse-vered with Robertson. At first sight he could have been the bloody groundsman rather than the outside-left who was going to make one of the goals and score the other that won the club those two European Cups in consecu-tive seasons. He was out of condition, overweight, ate too many chips, smoked too many fags, and the unshaven chin made him look as scruffy as the clothes he wore. If there was a player in the entire League who was slower than this lad and looked less like a professional footballer, I never saw him. Yet if you think David Beckham is fairly handy with his right foot, you should have seen the way

Robbo eventually crossed a ball with his left – or his right if need be!

There was some indefinable quality about this Scottish scruff that persuaded me to think he might just be worth a chance. It certainly wasn't his initial attitude, which sometimes made me want to cry, but it might have had something to do with the fact that he could make you laugh.

So let's look at O'Neill and Robertson, let's see where the managerial expertise comes from. The easy answer is to say that they couldn't have worked with Taylor and me for so long without some of the magic rubbing off. I sure hope it did. One thing's for certain, they'd have had to be as thick as planks not to have learned something, picked up the odd tip or home truth here and there, and neither of them is thick.

O'Neill's intelligence was clear to me the moment I was confronted by him at Forest. He was bright, highly charged-up even on the field, hyper-active almost. If there was one player I clashed with more than any other during my time in management, it was Martin O'Neill. I think management has given him the platform on which he can display his intelligence.

He had an opinion on almost anything and was never slow to express it, not unlike the young Clough, I suppose, in the dressing room and on the training field at Middlesbrough all those years ago. He definitely had an inflated value of his own playing ability and I was constantly having to put him straight about that. No, he wasn't Stanley Matthews and Tom Finney rolled into one – he just thought he was. Whenever he was left out of the side at Forest his frustration used to boil over and pour out of him; he couldn't control it.

He had the ability to communicate better than most. He had been clever enough to go to university and gain qualifications and he repeatedly hung this over me like the sword of Damocles. That made me furious on two counts – a) I wasn't on his level, academically, and b) I didn't want it ramming down my throat every time he didn't appear on the teamsheet. He had to learn that I ran the show – it was as simple as that.

Of course he will have learned along the way. His intelligence, his knowledge of football and the way players behave and react, his ability and his willingness to display it for the manager he hardly regarded as his best friend – all of it would have been part of the learning process. He took his first steps into management with Grantham, and then, with so much success, Wycombe. He was briefly at Norwich and spectacularly at Leicester. That intelligence of his convinced him that he shouldn't replace me when I retired at the City Ground and that the Celtic job was the perfect calling after he'd taken Leicester just about as far as they are likely to go.

He'll have learned one of his sharpest lessons on 12 August 1978, not the Glorious Twelfth for Martin as things turned out although he did score two of the five goals we put past Ipswich in the Charity Shield at Wembley. I hauled him off. If he'd thought I was against him before that day, he must have been absolutely certain when I made my decision to substitute him. Two goals to his name and he wanted to be a bigger hero still. He wanted a bloody hat-trick.

'Gerrim off,' I snapped at Jimmy Gordon alongside me on the Wembley bench.

'You can't do it.'

'Can't I? If you don't get O'Neill off that pitch right now, I'll sack you.'

It was unusual to talk to Jimmy like that. Given our background at Middlesbrough – him among the senior professionals and me still wearing L plates – I regarded and treated him like my elder brother. I paid him as much respect as anybody ever paid any coach. Anyway, he did as I asked, or demanded, and O'Neill came off. He didn't say a word until after the match and then I knew it was coming.

'Why did you bring me off?'

'To save money for the FA,' I told him. 'The way the match was developing they'd have needed to chuck on an extra ball – one for everybody else as well as the one you were keeping to yourself.'

'Well,' he protested, 'I had got two goals.'

'I know – but you weren't going to get a third by playing on your own. That was a certainty and that's why you had to come off.'

Of course he didn't like it. Players never do like decisions that go against them, decisions that let them know the truth. But they do remember them and for any player contemplating a career in management, those are the decisions most worth remembering. O'Neill just wouldn't give the ball to anybody. He was after his third goal but in looking for it he had stopped playing for the team. We were playing Ipswich off the pitch. I don't know what the biggest score ever was for a Charity Shield but we were threatening to break all records. Nevertheless, even though victory was assured against a very accomplished side, O'Neill's selfishness still had to be eliminated in the wider interests of the team. It took him weeks and weeks to get over it.

There were many times when I clashed with him, usually when I left him out of the side, and I was forever hearing him moan, 'I might as well pack my bags and go back to university.' I heard it once too often and pulled him in front of all the other players.

'Martin,' I said, 'I've done you a big favour.'

'What's that, Boss?' It was a growl or a sulk more than the civilised tone I was entitled to from an educated young man.

'I've arranged that flight for you back to Ireland and I've organised a place at university. Get on it.'

He never mentioned university again. Eventually, despite our clashes, he did become an integral part of the side but, for somebody so bright, it surprised me that I had to teach him the game. He didn't know it at first, not properly. He finished up as second-highest goalscorer one season and he might have been our top scorer but he didn't know where those goals were coming from. He hadn't twigged, until I pointed it out, that most of those goals could be traced to the feet of John Robertson.

'Your goals are coming from the left. You're standing

there on your own when that ball comes to you because the opposition have been drawn to the magnet on our left-wing. That's why you're getting so many chances.'

I had to explain things like that to him. It took him a couple of years into his managerial career before he asked John Robertson, 'What was all that the gaffer used to shout at me – "Get the ball"? He used to shout it at me all the time and always after we'd scored.'

'If we had the ball, the other side hadn't got it,' Robbo replied. 'Simple as that.' Robbo had known what I meant.

Martin began to twig daft little things like that, familiar phrases and sayings he had heard from me almost on a day-to-day basis. It took him years to cotton on to the jargon and the importance of possession. A team can't play if it doesn't have the ball. He was puzzled by another regular cry from me in the dug-out. 'Stop that bloody ball going in the box,' I'd shout time after time. Robbo, I gather, had to explain, 'Where's the goal? In the penalty area. Well, if our team make sure the ball doesn't go into our box, there's a good chance it won't go in our net.'

It will all have become second nature to Martin by now. He will say things, do things, almost without thinking.

I'm certain he will still reflect from time to time on the day I denied him his place in the 1979 European Cup final. It was in Munich against Malmo, the Swedish champions. I'm sure Archie Gemmill still resents that big decision of mine because I left him out as well.

Everybody wants to play in a match like that. Players who are not fit will say they are, so, yet again, it all comes down to the judgement of the man in charge.

No decision was necessary as far as Frank Clark was concerned – he had been ruled out already – but O'Neill and Gemmill had been trying to work off their injuries and insisted they were fine. Not in my book, they weren't. They were doing what I would have done as a player in the same circumstances. I would have insisted I was fit even if I couldn't walk, let alone run. They were borderline but my hunch was not to risk either of them so I told them they were out. Hard decisions have to be taken. They're the ones that separate good managers from rotten managers.

We were sitting on the grass that day, me squatting on a football with all the players in front of me. I made sure none of them had the chance to sneak up behind me and kick the ball away because that had happened to me before and it bloody well hurts your backside. Archie insisted he was 'absolutely perfect' and, if I remember correctly, Martin answered my inquiry about his fitness by saying, 'I'm as right as rain, Gaffer.'

'Oh,' I said, 'I'm absolutely delighted. So everybody's fit. Smashing. But you two are not playing.'

They thought I was kidding. They both had hamstring problems and ought to have known what was coming – those rules again. If somebody had a hamstring problem and said he was fit, I invariably ordered two more weeks' rest. I'd have a word with the physio on a Thursday and if he said the lad was fit, I would still order another couple of weeks. It meant missing one more match but two weeks was invaluable for anybody recovering from an injury.

Archie's response was typical of the miserable little bugger – little, perhaps, but big enough to take the disappointment. He said something like, 'Fuck you, then. If you're not playing me, you're not playing me.' I know what Martin said – nothing. Again, it took him weeks to get over it. He avoided me at every opportunity but once our victory celebrations were over back home, it was the close season and he was away playing for Northern Ireland – not a lot, mind, because he broke down with, you've guessed it, a hamstring problem.

He got his resentment out of his system during the summer. He needed to because he had enough to worry about, trying to convince me he was worth a place in my team the following season. He managed it twenty-eight times in the League but scored just three goals, the same number, would you believe, as Larry Lloyd – the lumbering centre-half. We surrounded Lloyd with people who could play and got so much out of him that he finished up in the England team again only to make a balls of it and not get selected again.

Martin was fit enough, and had obviously done enough, for me to pick him for that second European Cup final in Madrid against Kevin Keegan's lot, Hamburg. It was before that game that he and the rest of them learned an unorthodox but effective way of preparing a football team for a big event. There are times, particularly at the end of a long, hard season, when players have had enough of training. What they want most is a break, time to relax and put their feet up. I'll bet Martin remembers well enough what we did in the week prior to beating Hamburg at the Bernabeu Stadium. I'm sure he learned the value of that lovely little break in Cala Millor, busy doing nothing. They were given no orders other than to relax completely and behave like responsible professionals. There was to be no training, no deadlines, no booze restrictions, providing they had a good lie-in to sleep off any hangover and didn't bother me with their bad heads.

You can spot the players who've done their bit in a full season just by looking at their faces – pale, hollow-cheeked and with eyes deep in their sockets. A beer is a better proposition than a ball for them at a time like that. I know one thing, my team welcomed the return of a ball to their feet that night in the Spanish capital. Despite injuries that cost us the services of Trevor Francis, whose header had won us the trophy a year earlier, we saw off Keegan and his new mates. We overcame the suffocating heat and we retained European football's most prestigious trophy thanks to the only goal of an ordinary game – from John Robertson's right foot.

There was a controversial aftermath and O'Neill and Robertson were in the middle of it. They were among the bunch who defied my refusal to let them leave the team hotel and travel miles into Madrid to join the wives and girlfriends and club staff who were staying in the city. I wasn't having Forest's sense of togetherness broken by anybody, especially on an occasion like that. My decision to take their winners' medals away from them couldn't have stuck but I was very close to doing it anyway. You can't have players defying your instructions, not even when they've just conquered Europe, so they had to be fined.

It was all part of the learning process that some absorb and others don't. I knew that O'Neill would stay in football because he was absorbing everything and it was clear to me that he would have too much to offer for the game to let him go. This was not an individual who would hang up his boots and disappear, not after living with me for a few years and all the tips he must have picked up. I also knew those who wouldn't make it if ever they tried their hand at management. Frank Clark was one, despite him making an impression at Leyton Orient, and taking over from me at Forest and putting them back in the Premiership for a spell. Once he took his boots off he reverted back to being Frank, strumming his guitar and smiling. We loved him – everybody loved Frank Clark – but management, certainly team management, just wasn't in him as far as I could see. He is far better suited to the administrative side of the business.

Trevor Francis was another. I've often described him as being too nice a bloke to be a manager. Also, if he was good at one thing apart from playing, it was crossing the 't's and dotting the 'i's on contracts. He always seemed to get a longer contract than anybody else.

There's nothing worse than a great performer losing some of his public appeal when he puts on a different hat. Francis in management was like watching Frank Sinatra attempting to become a juggler and dropping the balls all over the stage. Trevor didn't need to think all that much as a player because he could run like the wind, cross a ball at full pace and get his fair share of goals. He wasn't injured all that much because he was so quick and so nimble. But none of those attributes were of any use to him in management. Where's he been? He was at Queens Park Rangers, then spent four years at Sheffield Wednesday where he didn't do too badly, especially in Cup competitions. Then there was Birmingham. He was at St Andrews for nearly six years without getting them promoted to the Premiership. Steve Bruce managed it at the first attempt after Trevor had gone. He not only got them there but has managed to keep them in the top division against considerable odds. He's bought well and organised them well and a bit of the Alex Ferguson motivation method must have rubbed off. Poor Trevor Francis, meanwhile, switched clubs with Bruce and went to Crystal Palace. But he's lost that job as well which came as no great surprise to me. So he's had a few years, here and there, and I think we're still waiting for him to prove he can be a top-notch manager.

Martin O'Neill was a man of the world in a young man's clothes. He had an awareness of life beyond his years; his awareness of football couldn't fail to develop while he worked with me and once he put his own interpretation of management into practice. He started at Grantham out of necessity. He was hardly likely to have the big clubs clamouring because he wasn't exactly the biggest name in the game. Without being derogatory or rude, Northern Irish international caps are not the be-all and end-all. Martin had sixty-four of them by the time we'd finished with him and he'd ended his playing days via Norwich, Manchester City and Notts County. Gaining an Irish cap is not quite like climbing Everest. The scarcity of players meant the good ones tended to be capped a great deal. Apart from his caps and the bit of glory he gained with Forest, he wasn't that well known within the game.

It wasn't planned, the Grantham job. It wasn't a case of 'I'll start at the bottom and work my way up.' There's another comparison with me – I didn't plan going into management at Hartlepools, either. It's a bit like a drowning man. If you can't swim, you grab anything. I grabbed Hartlepools, Martin clutched Grantham and we both survived – eventually to look back and be glad that we learned our trade at the foot of the ladder. He has also reached the top because that's what happens with talent.

His ability began to show itself at Wycombe, the little club he led into the Football League and swept to promotion. It was inevitable that Forest would want him as my successor but I understood perfectly when he rejected the chance. He would have weighed up the pros and cons. Not many people would have wanted to follow me, anyway, particularly at Forest who were never what you would call a big club. To think that as a player I was watched by 30,000 people at Notts County but I couldn't get 30,000 to come to watch Forest even in a semi-final of the European Cup.

Martin would have weighed everything up, knowing that it would be one long battle at the City Ground, and finished up going to another East Midlands club after an extremely short spell at Norwich. He went to Leicester – a similar club to Forest only worse. They have never struck me as the most ambitious of clubs either, but Martin did what all promising managers do. He held his own. Then he took them to the Premiership and into Europe having won the Worthington Cup twice – the one they used to call the League Cup, the trophy we won so many times at Forest that we regarded it as much our property as the tea-urn in the guest room.

He'd had John Robertson alongside him all the way from Grantham. They were always mates as players. When I arrived at Forest they had something else in common apart from being on the transfer list – neither of them was in the team. Some people raised their eyebrows when they paired-up in non-league management in Maggie Thatcher's home town. I didn't. When you enter an unknown world, which management was to Martin O'Neill, irrespective of the club or the level, you take someone you know. You take a pal. Just like I took Peter Taylor, Martin O'Neill took his best mate.

If you ever need someone to relax with – and there

are countless times in football management when the need for relaxation is vital – I can think of few better companions than Robertson. Sometimes a manager needs to switch off, even if it's only for five minutes over a cup of coffee, and you need to feel safe because there are too many occasions when you are consumed by panic. If you have never experienced real panic, I can tell you it is not a pleasant feeling at all.

Football management can be a torment, even to those who are deservedly regarded as the best. All it takes is a difficult spell, a poor run of results, a lousy season and sometimes you don't know which door to walk through, who to shout at or clout, which pen to pick up, which bell to push, which player to pick, which telephone to answer. Panic. Then John Robertson walks in. Panic over. He can evaporate it like a magician. He would have made a good street performer. He'd just amble up with a fag in his mouth and change the atmosphere, the entire environment, almost without knowing it. He could dry tears, make sad people happy and complaining people realise how lucky they really were. He would make you smile, relax you completely and it wouldn't take longer than five minutes. He is one of that rare breed of men who can cheer you up without trying. Honest, you couldn't fall out with John Robertson if he was knocking off your wife!

Pete Taylor was another who could change your mood from depression to delight, lethargy to laughter, in a trice. Taylor was more of a hardened professional than Robertson but as relaxation therapists, if that's an appropriate term for somebody who spreads laughter, they are exactly the same. It's another oddity of life that Taylor and I should fall out over Robbo when Pete nicked him and took him to Derby. It was a stupid reason for not talking until it was too late but there it is, another reason for regret. When we were still on speaking terms, Pete had said to me on several occasions, 'Bye, but it's a bloody lonely job, in't it?' I'll tell you this, with all his success at Celtic, winning the Scottish title two years on the trot, there would have been times when O'Neill felt lonely. He'll have felt far less lonely thanks to Robbo being around. It's helped him seize the big chance.

Martin did have one thing going for him when he arrived up there in Glasgow – he didn't need to work too hard to get fans to come to the ground. All he had to do was tell them it's a Saturday! What a luxury, massive home crowds virtually guaranteed. The crowds are absolutely guaranteed these days because O'Neill and Robertson have done their stuff, and in a way not dissimilar to the way they did it at Leicester. They spot talent others seem to be unaware of; they know what the team needs and how and where to buy replacements without always having to pay a fortune; and they get the best out of the squad they've assembled. That's management. That's what Peter Taylor and I did as a partnership – not always with the approval of our employers or the establishment but always knowing exactly why we were doing it.

The example of John Robertson is an important one

in all this. As I've said, he didn't look anything like a professional athlete when I first clapped eyes on him. In fact, there were times when he barely resembled a member of the human race. He's the only man I've ever known who insisted on wearing suede shoes even when there was no suede visible to the naked eye. They were so old, shabby little bits of leather that used to be suede shoes, but he wore them week in, week out. They became a household joke at the City Ground. Taylor used to hold them up in the dressing room. It was all he needed to do to have everybody laughing. Robbo's trousers never fitted him either. He had trousers with flared bottoms before they were invented, and he had big legs for such a short lad. But we're talking about one of the most talented footballers I ever saw.

What God gave him was the same dimensions all the way down from his neck. His neck, his chest, his stomach, his thighs and his calves were all the same size! If you'd melted him down and he lost weight from everywhere – a bit from his calves, a bit from his thighs, a bit from his middle – he would have been three stone lighter but exactly the same shape.

You should have seen him get on the coach. He didn't jump on or spring on with the air and surefootedness of an athlete; he waddled up to it, put his left foot first on the bottom step and was the only player to use the handrails to help himself through the door. Oh yeah, and you'd occasionally see him squash his fag under his other foot. He used to think I hadn't seen him smoking. I didn't have to see him – I could smell him from the other end of the car park. To think this was the player who won two European Cups – the first with that left-footed cross for Trevor Francis's header and the second with his own right-footed winner.

Robbo and O'Neill roomed together with Forest whenever possible. Sometimes I split everybody up as part of the blending process. It served two purposes. It helped the sense of togetherness – after all, we relied on each other on matchdays so it was as well that everybody got on. Secondly, it helped me assert my authority. Once they realised they had to do what I told them, it solved a million possible problems.

So there you have them, Martin O'Neill and John Robertson, the academic and the scruff, the Irishman and the Scotsman, chalk and cheese just like Peter Taylor and me. Right now they look like being the best managerial twosome in the British game, odds-on to take over at Manchester United eventually, I'd say. They've a bit to do yet, especially in Europe, because providing you beat Rangers a few times, the Scottish title is not the most difficult thing in the world to win. I know they won't have tried to copy Pete and me because neither of them is that barmy. They're not the new Clough and Taylor because nobody can be and they wouldn't want to be. What I do hope is that Pete and I contributed something towards the success they are enjoying and I'm sure will continue to enjoy. I hope we gave them some idea. I like to think we helped. We must have done. Just a little bit.

C H A P T E R 9

BOTTLES AND BUFFOONS

At Nottingham Forest, we rarely did things like anybody else. They used to say I was never at the ground and never at the training ground. Where do people pick up garbage like that? One of my proudest achievements in management was that sequence of forty-two matches. We were undefeated from November 1978 when we lost 1–0 at Leeds through to December 1979 when we lost 2–0 at Liverpool. A run like that from a team that was to end the season with three trophies, including the one Fergie didn't win in Glasgow, would surely be worth a knighthood these days, at the very least. The format has changed now with fewer matches in the Premiership than we had to play in the old first division, but it will be an awfully long time before anybody gets close to equalling that extraordinary record of ours.

It wasn't done on the strength of filling players'

minds with technical and tactical jargon or coaching gobbledygook. It was done by keeping everything as simple as possible, by keeping minds neat and tidy and free from clutter. It was done by making sure that whatever the situation, however daunting the next match might look, Nottingham Forest would be represented by good players who were relaxed. Fear? If I ruled my club with anything, it was relaxation!

That's why we had beer on the coach during the journey to Munich's Olympic stadium for that 1979 final against Malmo. OK, so it turned out to be a fairly crappy encounter apart from the Robertson cross that set up Trevor Francis's winning header, but Forest's footballers weren't uptight footballers when they took the field. What's wrong with a beer or two *en route* to the ground? It was better than sitting there bored to a stupor watching a bloody video of opponents who weren't as good as us even though we were one or two players short of our best side.

Forest did a lot of smiling in those days. As you may know, the following season we took them to the red-light district in Amsterdam before the semi-final with Ajax. Pete Taylor's attempts to organise a discount for twenty-odd players and officials didn't quite work but the effect did. I don't think anybody seriously wanted to watch one of those notorious live shows but the laughter that followed Taylor's attempted negotiations was more valuable to my side than anything they could have taught us at Lilleshall.

We were unconventional to say the least but boredom

was something we wanted to avoid at all costs even though, on occasions, the unorthodox approach had its price. Like one pre-season trip to Holland where I took the players to a kind of fitness club with swimming pool, saunas, all that kind of stuff. It was just a knock-about session, something to break the daily routine, something to do rather than train. It all seemed a very good idea at the time until a member of the coaching staff reported that one player had damaged his ankle and another had all but broken his wrist. Both had slipped, clambering out of the jacuzzi! A slight hitch to the pre-session planning although we didn't let it bother us too much.

They were together; I think it's called 'bonding' in modern parlance. Whatever it was, we won all three games on that tour.

On another occasion, before one of our League Cup finals, I had half-a-dozen bottles of champagne put into ice-buckets as I joined a card school with some of the players. You can get carried away playing cards. When Jimmy Gordon marched in and announced, 'Do you lot realise it's ten o'clock?' I said, 'It feels as if we've only just arrived.' Jimmy wasn't slow or afraid to express his opinion and said, 'We've been here since six. Surely you're not starting with bridge schools at this time. The players certainly aren't staying up all night.'

'Get the champagne open,' was my response.

'No, it's too late for that as well.'

'How come?' I argued. 'Have all the staff gone to bed? You get hold of the manager – he can open it.'

'It's not that, but Archie Gemmill's already gone to bed.'

'Well go and get him up, then.'

'He's asleep,' Jimmy said. 'I can't do that.'

But he did. It was an instruction from the gaffer but it was the usual grumpy Gemmill who reluctantly joined us, refused a drink and complained, 'This is ridiculous. Getting us out of bed when we're preparing for a League Cup final.'

Now he had a point, of course, but he was isolating himself and his mood offended me.

'It's going to be a long night,' I told him, 'because everybody is staying right here until you drink that glass of champagne.'

He sat me out until gone half past eleven. The lads had had maybe a glass and a half each. I think it was Kenny Burns who said, 'I'm ready for bed, Gaffer,' and then turning to Gemmill, said, 'If you don't drink that bloody champagne, I'm going to choke you with it.'

Archie swigged it down in one and everybody was in bed within five minutes. For better, for worse, those were the kind of things we used to do; and, nearly always, it was for the better. I couldn't understand the song and dance that was made about England players playing cards and watching horse racing at the 2000 European Championship. For a start, I don't believe some of the figures that were bandied about – tens of thousands of pounds on the table.

However, I played cards with the players both at Derby and at Forest, and for money. There was nothing sinister or serious about it and I'm not aware that it ever caused the slightest ripple of a problem among the players. But it's not valid to compare what England did and what I used to do as a manager because players' wages haven't just increased, they have gone through the roof. The highest-paid player at Derby was probably on about forty quid a week and at Forest on £200 to £250. The married players looked after their cash, and the single players – well, they had more money to play with. As for me, I was earning £22,000 a year at Derby, the highest salary of all. I had a rule that nobody got more money than me because I was the manager.

It wasn't the players' card schools and televised horse racing that was the problem for Keegan at Euro 2000. It was what happened on the field, not off it. Too little happened on the field if truth be known, and he didn't seem to know what to do about it. How the memories came flooding back when Keegan resigned from the very job that I had wanted more than any other – manager of England. Who was better qualified in 1977 after Don Revie turned his back and fled to Dubai, lured by the money? The offer from the United Arab Emirates had been made with perfect timing because England's results were not turning out as Revie had hoped they would. I was not only ready for the job, I was perfect for it because I would have been good at it.

Time has done nothing to change my view that, had Revie's successor been selected on the strength of the interviews carried out in London, the job would have been mine – mine and Peter Taylor's because I would certainly have insisted that he was appointed as well.

I didn't have a challenger apart from Bobby Robson who never did win the league championship at Ipswich but was always likely to become national manager somewhere along the line – and did when he was better equipped for the job. Lawrie McMenemy's main claim to fame had been winning the FA Cup with Southampton and keeping them in the first division. No disrespect to Lawrie but anybody can win a Cup with a bit of luck – it's only six ties for a club from the top division.

Lawrie was to wear that cherished FA blazer with the three lions on the breast pocket as Graham Taylor's assistant after the Robson regime. Dear Lawrie, a fellow Northeasterner – I don't think he kicked a ball as a professional footballer. He completed his apprenticeship as a manager at Doncaster and Grimsby and, funnily enough, worked as a coach for my old mentor Alan Brown at Sheffield Wednesday. He finished up getting a lot closer to the England manager's job than I did, even though the other contenders on the short list I think shouldn't have been contenders at all – director of coaching Allen Wade and Charlie Hughes.

When I sit at home, busy doing not a great deal at all, and think back again to that day I bowled into Lancaster Gate as if I already owned the place, I remain unshakeable in my belief that the whole interviewing process was a charade. It wouldn't have made the slightest difference one way or the other because the England job was already earmarked for a man who wasn't even on the list of those to be interviewed. Ron Greenwood had been standing in since Revie quit. It was done and dusted, decided near as damn it before the FA lot got down to talking to Bobby, Lawrie and the candidate who was best qualified of all – me.

Greenwood had a good name in the game as manager of the West Ham side that included Bobby Moore, Martin Peters and Geoff Hurst, three of the Boys of '66. He was generally described as one of the most knowledgeable and respected of all coaches and I'm sure he was although I remain baffled by the fact that he couldn't decide who was the better goalkeeper – Peter Shilton from our place or Ray Clemence from Liverpool. They were both the same according to Greenwood, so he alternated, picking first one then the other. They might call it rotation today but as far as I was concerned it was indecision way back then, an instance of a manager who couldn't make a positive choice – clear evidence of uncertainty and a lack of emphatic judgement.

I wasn't comfortable with most of the company at that interview. Many of them are now dead, of course. The panel included Professor Sir Harold Thompson who hadn't a clue about my business; Bert Millichip, since knighted, who couldn't have been my biggest fan after some of the things I'd said about the way they did things at his club, West Brom; Peter Swales who promised me his vote; and Dick Wragg from Sheffield who promised everybody he'd buy them lunch the next time they happened to be in his town. I had nothing in common with any of them so you can imagine how grateful I was to see Sir Matt Busby sitting there. He knew my business; he knew what made a manager. He must have known I was the best man for the job and maybe his vote was the only one I received. It didn't come from Swales, the bloke who said I could bank on his support. See what I mean? Football directors!

They could have saved us all a lot of time and bother because Greenwood seemed merely to be rubber-stamped. He was given the job and most of those silly committee men would have gone home and boasted to their wives and friends, in-laws and golf-club cronies, that they had appointed that nice Ron Greenwood, a first-class diplomat as well as a fine coach, and they had given the bum's rush to that objectionable braggart from Nottingham Forest.

What they didn't know and couldn't have told their cronies at that stage was that the braggart from Nottingham was about to embark on a period of his career that would lead Nottingham Forest to the league championship, two League Cup triumphs, two European Cups and the European Super Cup – oh, and that little matter of forty-two league games unbeaten, in the process – all in less than three years. Who could object to that? I think England's supporters might just have welcomed having a braggart in charge of the team.

The way England managers are appointed still puzzles me and sometimes keeps me awake at night. It frustrates and annoys me – I become vitriolic, furious. When I think of the power they have, I shudder. It's not the power of an American president, perhaps, the man with his finger on the nuclear button. What they don't tell you is that the button was disconnected some time ago in case daft buggers like Ronald Reagan or Bill Clinton pressed it at the wrong time.

The selection process seems to lack plenty in the way of professional knowledge and expertise. It's changed to some extent in that one or two professionals have been consulted, but I gather the appointment of Sven-Goran Eriksson, the first foreign coach in charge of the England team, was mainly down to the FA's chief executive Adam Crozier. Isn't this the man from the world of advertising or some such? And isn't he a Scotsman? Now I'm not being racist or prejudiced in any way. Eriksson might turn out to be the best manager England ever had. It's just that I would have preferred it if an Englishman rather than a Scotsman had been appointing the England manager, and preferably an Englishman steeped in the game – a former player and manager together with other former players and managers or people with sound experience and judgement that could not be questioned.

How could those, apart from Sir Matt Busby, who pretended to interview me seriously for their job ignore such credentials and public support? I'll tell you. It's the reason why Len Shackleton left a blank page in his autobiography to illustrate how much such people know about the game.

I wanted the England job because I knew I'd be good at it. But I shouldn't have been walking into what felt like an alien environment. I should have been walking in there like a vicar entering his church to meet the bishops. He wouldn't have felt out of place because he was joining people of the same persuasion and way of life; he'd have felt comfortable. Instead, despite my confidence, despite telling them England had enough good players to win trophies, I was still made to feel like an outsider.

Even if Ron Greenwood hadn't been favourite, I think that conceit of mine would have cost me the England job – the way I walked into the interview room giving the impression that I felt superior to everybody else there. Apart from Matt Busby, I was of course, but you'd be amazed at the reaction of some people in those circumstances. I'm sure one or two of them were saying to themselves, 'Who the hell does this man think he is, walking in here like that?' When you are conceited, when you are full of yourself and oozing confidence, you are completely unaware of the effect it has on others.

That interview has occupied my thoughts a lot since I finished with football and I'm convinced I made one serious mistake that gave the committee the ideal opportunity to push me to one side. Me and my big mouth! Sir Matt asked if I was serious when I told them I would take anything they cared to offer, any job they might have in mind. They seized the opportunity to chuck me the booby prize. They gave me the chance to get involved with the England youth team and, as you might imagine, Taylor and I jumped in with both feet. Not content simply to observe during a tournament in

Las Palmas, as was expected of us, we took over. I couldn't stand the sight of the coach, a man by the name of Ken Burton, running the show like an amateur. It was as if reaching the final was enough for the FA bods who had travelled out there. The Russian side was expected to win the tournament anyway. When that team of ours walked out of the dressing room there was no feeling of inferiority, I can tell you. Whatever else I did on that little trip, I made sure that the England lads knew they had every right to be contesting that final against the youngsters from Russia. The only goal of the match gave that youth side their first tournament victory since God knows when – satisfying, for all that our involvement had been fairly limited. Taylor and I had made our point, but it was not a job for us long term. It was no compensation for missing out on the big one so we jacked it in after a year or so and concentrated all our efforts on making history with Nottingham Forest.

I've been asked a million times, and asked myself on a few occasions, why I would have made a good England manager. Time to dwell has only increased my certainty that I would have been successful. I already had a bond with the players. Those people who might question whether my style of management would have worked at international level are entitled to their opinion. I don't mind them having an opinion just as long as they realise that mine is better informed than theirs.

Those players knew I had been one of them for a longish period of my life. Even the dim ones will have known that I used to be a centre-forward, and a bloody good 'un, so the respect would have been immediate. Centre-forward, or striker in today's language, remains the most difficult position on the field. Has there ever been a single football match in the entire history of the game after which somebody hasn't said 'he should have put that one away' or 'we could have won the game if he hadn't missed that sitter'? There's always a scoring chance made in a football match and it's nearly always the bloke up front who carries the burden. So my record as a player would have helped me, and for those who weren't aware of it I'd have probably plastered it on the dressing room wall at Wembley.

Also, I knew most of the better players in the country. I'd worked with some of them. They would have enjoyed my verbal approach to the job. I'm not being flippant but if I told one of them to 'piss off' he'd recognise the language and, after a period of time, would know that I meant it. They would have understood all my terminology, on and off the training ground.

I would have known who were the good players and who were the ones who didn't have a prayer of getting a place in my England team. You would be staggered by the number of managers who don't know their best team. Even the worst manager might get nine names right but it's the other two who can make the difference between a poor team and a winning one. I keep going back to Ron Greenwood and the problem he had in deciding between the merits of Peter Shilton and Ray Clemence – and he was the man who landed the job I went for!

I had established that the goalkeeper is as important as anyone else on the field, if not more important than some. Goalkeepers used to be regarded as a bit of a joke. Anybody could get a goalkeeper. They didn't attract big money. I paid £270,000 to Stoke for Shilton because I knew that with him behind that team at Forest there were no limits on the scope of their potential. I decided what Ron Greenwood couldn't decide to save his life. I decided Peter Shilton was the best keeper in England. No disrespect to Clemence whatsoever but, in my judgement, Shilton was just that little bit better.

So, being on the right wavelength and starting with the best keeper of all as the first name on my teamsheet, I would have been a tenth of the way there. Hey, I'd have had the finest footballers in the country available to me. We'd have had a lot of fun together. It would have been the most relaxed England set-up of all time. We would have had a colourful team, playing the type of football the public wants to see, and it would have been winning football as well. Oh, I might have had to tone down the language on occasions when the FA were within earshot but I'm a players' man and the England lads would have known it. As for missing the day-to-day involvement of club football, I would have relished the prospect of working with the best in the land once every three months or so. We would have been as fresh as daisies every time we got together. So don't tell me I would have failed as England manager. I'll never believe it for a second. Me? Working with the best of the very best? I couldn't have failed.

IN TRIBUTE

'I remember watching his teams play and that Forest
side of the late-1970s will go down in history as one of
the all-time greats. I was truly touched when he com-
plimented the way this current Arsenal side plays and
said that we deserved to break his record. People use
the word legend too freely, but Brian Clough is a true
legend of English football. His success in this country
and in Europe is a legacy for which he will always be
remembered.'
Arsene Wenger, Arsenal manager

'He was absolutely sensational and I don't think Brian
would disagree. He was England's version of Muham-
mad Ali, a more charismatic man you could not meet. He
had everything. We were extremely lucky to work with
someone so talented and so brilliant. One of the great

myths about him was that he was a manager and not a coach, and seldom on the training ground. The truth is that every day was a coaching lesson from Brian. In a 25-minute spell, you would pick up enough to last you a lifetime. People ask you to recount a Brian Clough story but the truth is every day with him was a Brian Clough story with each one better than the last. God, he will be badly missed.'

Martin O'Neill, Celtic manager and former Forest player

'He was a fantastic manager. All his teams were difficult to beat and always had a determination about them, like the man himself. To win back-to-back European Cups with Nottingham Forest has to go down as one of the finest managerial achievements of all time.'

Sir Alex Ferguson, Manchester United manager

'He would have ruffled a few feathers and disturbed the corridors of power but I think he would have been a good England manager. He had good judgement, knew how to design a team and was a great motivator.'

Sir Bobby Robson, former England manager

'Brian was a teacher, he taught players how to pass, and told them to keep the ball on the floor and to respect authority. He was one of the greatest teachers of players the game has ever seen. If I ever need memories of Brian I just have to look at my medal cabinet – it's full of them.'

John McGovern, former Forest captain